THE TRANSCRIPTS

CHINESE SAYINGS
BOOK 3

LASZLO MONTGOMERY

Chinese Sayings Book 3

By Laszlo Montgomery

Trade Paper: 978-988-8904-29-7
Digital: 978-988-8904-28-0

© 2025 Laszlo Montgomery

HISTORY / Asia / China

EB229

All rights reserved. No part of this book may be reproduced in material form, by any means, whether graphic, electronic, mechanical or other, including photocopying or information storage, in whole or in part. May not be used to prepare other publications without written permission from the publisher except in the case of brief quotations embodied in critical articles or reviews. For information contact info@earnshawbooks.com

Published in Hong Kong by Earnshaw Books Ltd.

CONTENTS

Author's Foreword	IX
Episode 1 A Swan Feather From A Thousand Li Away 千里送鹅毛—Qiān Lǐ Sòng É Máo	1
Episode 2 Invite the Gentleman Into the Urn 请君入瓮—Qǐng Jūn Rù Wèng	9
Episode 3 Betting The Bank 孤注一掷—Gū Zhù Yī Zhì	15
Episode 4 Double Sorrow 人琴俱亡—Rén Qín Jù Wáng	23
Episode 5 Whole Lotta Love 琴瑟和鸣—Qín Sè Hè Míng	29
Episode 6 Create Your Destiny 乘风破浪—Chéng Fēng Pò Làng	37
Episode 7 Two Faced Back Stabber 口蜜腹剑—Kǒu Mì Fù Jiàn	43
Episode 8 A Farcical Ending 狗尾續貂—Gǒu Wěi Xù Diāo	49
Episode 9 The Wood Man 木人石心—Mù Rén Shí Xīn	59
Episode 10 You Asked For It 开门揖盗—Kāi Mén Yī Dào	69

Episode 11 Life is But a Dream   77
黄粱美梦—Huáng Liáng Měi Mèng

Episode 12 Do As I Say, Not As I Do   89
只许州官放火,不许百姓点灯—zhǐ xǔ zhōu guān fàng huǒ, bù xǔ bǎi xìng diǎn dēng

Episode 13 Sweating Buckets   97
汗流浃背—Hàn Liú Jiā Bèi

Episode 14 The Comeback Kid   105
东山再起—Dōng Shān Zài Qǐ

Episode 15 A Blessing in Disguise   115
塞翁失马—Sài Wēng Shī Mǎ

Episode 16 I Was Made to Love Her   121
家徒四壁—Jiā Tú Sì Bì

Episode 17 We Swore Blood Brothers Against The Wind   129
桃园结义—Táo Yuán Jié Yì

Episode 18 I Carry the Burden and Shame   137
忍辱負重—Rěn Rǔ Fù Zhòng

Episode 19 All I Want Is To Be Next To You   145
近水楼台—Jìn Shuǐ Lóu Tái

Episode 20 She's A Woman   151
巾帼英雄—Jī Guó Yīng Xióng

Episode 21 Blue, Blue, My World is Blue   157
青出于蓝—Qīng Chū Yú Lán

Episode 22 Shock The Monkey   163
树倒猢狲散—Shù Dǎo Hú Sūn Sàn

Episode 23 Don't Count Me Out Yet   173
大器晚成—Dà Qì Wǎn Chéng

Episode 24 The Truth Always Gets Out   181
东窗事发—Dōng Chuāng Shì Fā

Episode 25 R-E-S-P-E-C-T   187
程门立雪—Chéng Mén Lì Xuě

Episode 26 Had Enough Yet?   195
七擒孟获—Qī Qín Mèng Huò

Episode 27 The First Cut is The Deepest   203
剪不断，理还乱—Jiǎn Bù Duàn, Lǐ Hái Luàn

Episode 28 You Can Get It If You Really Want (But You Must Try)   211
磨杵成针—Mó Chǔ Chéng Zhēn

Episode 29 Finished Behind The Last Place Guy   217
名落孙山—Míng Luò Sūn Shān

AUTHOR'S FOREWORD

I'm thrilled to present to you the second in a series of three books containing Chinese "chengyu" idioms.

Like the Chinese Sayings in Book 1 of the series, these are all derived from ancient and medieval classical literature, and stories rooted in history. Even though many of them are more than two thousand years old, they are still widely used in modern Chinese to convey something on the one hand complex but on the other hand somewhat profound. They are concise yet memorable.

One of the aspects of these Chinese Sayings is that their figurative meaning almost always could not be deduced simply by reading the four (or more) characters.

About five years after I launched the China History Podcast I thought that with these "chengyu" phrases so often rooted in history, why not launch a new podcast show that would introduce one chengyu per episode, whatever the origins of the idiom, be it a work of literature, folklore, official history, historical events, or philosophical text.

What's cool about these chengyu or Chinese Sayings is that they convey rich meanings, morals, and pearls of wisdom in a compact form, often summarizing a story or a moral lesson. Chengyu phrases add depth and nuance to the language.

Since I launched the Chinese Sayings Podcast, over 90 episodes have been produced as of late 2024. Both Cathay Pacific and Singapore Airlines carry these Chinese Sayings Podcast shows in their inflight entertainment systems.

In these anthologies being published by Earnshaw Books, the entirety of these famous and historic Chinese Sayings is being presented in three volumes. Each consists of my curated selections of the most engaging, relatable, and thought-provoking Chengyu-Chinese Sayings. No matter if you're a fluent Chinese speaker, in the process of learning or have never studied before, these books introduce you to a wonderful slice of Chinese culture that you can use in your daily life, at home, at the office, or out with your friends and family.

Here in Volume 2 of this 3-Part Chinese Sayings Anthology, chengyu idioms from the Warring States and Han Dynasty are featured. I hope you will enjoy and appreciate these cultural classics from more than two thousand years ago.

Laszlo Montgomery

Chinese Sayings Book 3
Episode 1

THE TRANSCRIPTS

A SWAN FEATHER FROM A THOUSAND LI AWAY

千里送鹅毛—Qiān Lǐ Sòng É Máo

TRANSCRIPT

00:00	Hello again everybody, this is Laszlo Montgomery here bringing you another nice chengyu for your personal collection. I'm not sure if today's Chinese Saying is my all-time favorite but it's right up there in the top five. Maybe even the top three.
00:17	Remember I said most all chengyu, or Chinese proverbs or idioms, are only four characters, four syllables long. Not this one. No, today's chengyu is five characters. Qiānlǐ sòng é'máo. 20% more syllables than usual. And there's a follow-up that goes along with this proverb that's also five characters long: lǐ qīng qíngyì zhòng. So, in toto, this one we're going to look at today is a whopping ten characters long.
00:50	Don't get too scared or too concerned. I assure you from decades of experience, if you just say the first five, that'll suffice in most all circumstances.

CHINESE SAYINGS BOOK 3
EPISODE 1

Qiānlǐ sòng é'máo. This one comes from a poem written during the Sòng Dynasty by the great statesman, literatus and calligrapher Ōuyáng Xiū 欧阳修, called Méi Shèng Yújì Yínxìng 梅圣俞寄银杏.

01:16 Let me break these characters down for you.

01:18 Qiān means a thousand.

Lǐ means a mile but specifically a Chinese mile which was about a third of a mile.

01:26 So, qiānlǐ means a thousand li or a thousand miles. The actual distance is not important. Qiānlǐ back in the 7th century was a long journey and not something undertaken lightly or on a whim.

01:41 Sòng means to send.

01:44 And É means a swan.

01:47 And máo means a feather. It's also the same character as in Máo Zedong. Chairman Máo.

01:49 So Qiānlǐ sòng é'máo. One thousand Li sent swan feather.

01:56 Once again, like most of these chengyu, these characters that are strung together don't appear to have any obvious meaning. Therefore there must be some story or something behind it that reveals the hidden meaning.

CHINESE SAYINGS BOOK 3
EPISODE 1

02:09 | And this is story behind these characters. It begins almost but not quite fourteen hundred years ago, the 7th century. The beginning of the fantastic and glorious Táng Dynasty. Well, not all of the Tang, but most of it. In past China History Podcast episodes we looked at one of the co-stars of our story today. This was the great Tàizōng Emperor. Táng Tàizōng.

02:39 | Now this Taizong emperor isn't the main character. Today's hero was an official from the region around Yúnnán and Burma. And his name was Miǎn Bógāo 缅伯高. This official was tasked by his king to go cozy up to the Tang emperor and to pay tribute and do what all states and kingdoms did back in those days, present gifts and bow before the Chinese emperor.

03:07 | So this land adjacent to Tang China where Miǎn Bógāo came from wanted to show their sincerity and devotion to the emperor. So this envoy, Miǎn Bógāo got all prepared for this long journey to the capital of China, the city of Chang'an. This is where modern day Xīān is.

03:28 | Now if you ask me, I think this official could have been chosen a different kind of gift to take to the Tàizōng emperor. But someone in all their wisdom and sagacity decided upon this beautiful snowy white swan as the primary gift. Perhaps there was something special about the white swans down in this part of southwest China and Burma.

03:50 | So off Miǎn Bógāo went, in a northerly direction, to the richest, largest, most spectacular city on Planet Earth at

3

CHINESE SAYINGS BOOK 3
EPISODE 1

that time, the city of Cháng'ān. He had this beautiful white swan placed in this travel basket and had everything he required for the journey packed up.

04:12   Now I'm not sure exactly from where he set out. But the journey he was about to take I'm estimating from around present day Kūnmíng in Yúnnán Province to Xian, that's about a thousand kilometers. About six hundred twenty miles. Well, off he went, swan and all, to go do his duty and shoeshine the emperor with this gift and make sure their little corner of the Far East stayed on China's good side.

04:41   He got as far as Húběi province, about halfway there. The most famous city in Húběi of course, is the city of Wǔhàn, right on the Yángzǐ River, longest river in China and third longest in the world. Also known in Hollywood as the Yang-Tze. There was a little town maybe a hundred kilometers away to the west of Wǔhàn called Xiāntáo 仙桃. And nearby was a lake, Lake Pai, Páihú 排湖. And right on the banks of this Páihú, Miǎn Bógāo took a breather and decided to allow the white swan to have a nice drink and at the same time he figured he'd give this swan a little wash and brighten him up a bit to his natural snowy white color.

05:25   Poor guy! With half the journey over, tragedy befell him. While he was trying to give this bird a bath, the swan saw an opening and escaped from Miǎn Bógāo's clutches and off he flew, gone in an instant leaving nothing behind except a single feather that floated back down to the water. Miǎn Bógāo took the feather in his

4

CHINESE SAYINGS BOOK 3
EPISODE 1

	hand and contemplated his predicament.
05:54	Etiquette dictated he couldn't show up empty-handed. But all he had left to offer was this one single feather.
06:02	So Miǎn Bógāo decided he'd just write a poem on a piece of silk that earnestly explained the circumstances and then he wrapped this swan feather in the silk and continued on his way. He arrived at the royal palace and had his big moment to kowtow before the Tàizōng emperor and to present his gift. And when the great Tàizōng emperor read the poem he was so delighted and moved by its sincerity and honesty, that he presented Miǎn Bógāo with gifts of silk, tea, jade and other royal baubles.
06:40	What Miǎn Bógāo said in his poem was that he was presenting a swan feather from a thousand Li away or a thousand miles away, if you will.
06:51	Then he followed these five characters up qiānlǐ sòng é'máo, with the second part, five more characters. Not only is this swan feather from a thousand miles away....
07:03	But also, Lǐ qīng, qíngyì Zhòng 礼轻情意重. A Lǐ is a gift. Qīng means light, as in weight. Qíngyì means affection or the positive feelings behind some action. And Zhòng means heavy. So Li Qing qingyi Zhong.
07:26	The gift is light, meaning it isn't much. But regardless of its lack of monetary value, the qíngyì, or the meaning behind it is zhòng, heavy, deep and profound.

CHINESE SAYINGS BOOK 3
EPISODE 1

07:38 | So Miǎn Bógāo in his poem presented to the great Táng Tàizōng said, here is a swan feather from a thousand Li away. The gift is a mere trifle but it represents great feelings and meaning from the people of that part of China where he came from.

07:56 | And as I said, this Tàizōng emperor, he got it. He understood what it all meant and was appropriately moved upon hearing the whole story, and as I said, he showered Miǎn Bógāo with the usual array of door prizes the emperor bestowed on those who came to bow before him and present gifts and pay tribute.

08:17 | So next time you pick up some tschotchke at some store that you wanted to give someone, if it's value is nothing special but you put a lot of thought into it, you can always say that this is a Qiānlǐ Sòng É'máo, Lǐ Qīng Qíngyì Zhòng. This is a swan feather from a thousand miles away, though the gift is a trifle, it conveys great meaning.

08:43 | But again, I want to reiterate if you just say Qiānlǐ Sòng É'máo you're totally okay. Someone who is a native speaker of Chinese knows the five characters that are supposed to follow. If you can't remember them, no big deal.

08:59 | So keep this one handy anytime you want to present a gift to anyone special in your life. The dollar value of the gift isn't that much. But the meaning behind the gift, the specialness, has great and profound meaning and therefore, value.

CHINESE SAYINGS BOOK 3
EPISODE 1

09:15 | Okay, that's going to be it for this time. Laszlo Montgomery signing off from Los Angeles and wishing you all my very best. Go check out our brother and sister podcasts: the China History Podcast and the Tea History Podcast. Those two and this exact same Chinese Sayings Podcast are all available at Teacup.Media. That's Teacup.media. Open 24/7 365 days per year.

09:42 | Take care everyone and please be my guest next time for another wholesome and satisfying episode of the Chinese Sayings Podcast.

Chinese Sayings Book 3
Episode 2

INVITE THE GENTLEMAN INTO THE URN

请君入瓮—Qǐng Jūn Rù Wèng

TRANSCRIPT

00:00 | Hey everyone, Laszlo Montgomery again, here with another nice chengyu for your Chinese Sayings collection. I hope everyone's finding these chéngyǔ's interesting and useful.

00:12 | This one today goes back to the Tang Dynasty, late 7th Century. This is another classic Chinese saying or chengyu. That is, it's four characters long and strung together into some kind of meaningless phrase which requires the knowledge about a certain story rooted in China's ancient past. Qǐng Jūn Rù Wèng. To invite the gentleman into the urn.

00:39 | Okay, let's do the usual and break down these four characters.

00:43 | Qǐng in this case means to invite.

00:46 | And a Jūn is a gentleman.

CHINESE SAYINGS BOOK 3
EPISODE 2

00:49 | Rù means into or to enter.

00:52 | And a Wèng is a kind of earthenware vase or urn. These can be very big. You could fit a person inside one.

01:00 | Qǐng Jūn Rù Wèng. Invite gentleman enter vase. Dang, if there's no story behind these four characters, I'll eat my hat.

01:13 | Well indeed there is. And it was written down in the Sòng Dynasty and comes to us straight from the Zīzhì Tōngjiàn 资治通鉴, the masterwork written by Sīmǎ Guāng 司马光 and a host of other scholars working almost two decades to produce the most authoritative history of China going back to the earliest times. In English it's often referred to as the "Comprehensive Mirror in Aid of Governance." In 1084 it was presented to the emperor Shénzōng 宋神宗.

01:42 | There's a scroll in the Zīzhì Tōngjiàn called the Táng Jì 唐记, the Annals of Tang. And in scroll number 121, there's this story about a gentleman named Zhōu Xìng 周兴. And his boss was none other than the only empress in all the thousands of years of Chinese history to rule in her own name as the empress of a dynasty. There were plenty of empress dowagers and regents but no one, not even the Empress Dowager Cíxǐ, could say they ruled and held the official top spot in the imperial government.

02:18 | Only one person had bragging rights to that claim to fame and that was the Empress Wǔ Zétiān. Our story takes place in the year 691. The year previous Wǔ Zétiān

CHINESE SAYINGS BOOK 3
EPISODE 2

had set up her fifteen-year Zhou Dynasty. It lasted until her death in 705. She was the only ruler in this dynasty. So in reality you can't really call it much of a dynasty.

02:44   Wǔ Zétiān was covered in another ancient podcast episode, so I won't go into details here. But suffice to say she had to step over a lot of dead bodies to get to where she ultimately ended up. She was ruthless and stopped at nothing to get what she wanted. When she finally had all her enemies neutralized she still maintained a very effective and feared secret police. Well, what secret police isn't feared.

03:13   And her guy, her secret police chief, was one of the true villains of Chinese history. Not very well known, but this police chief Lái Jùnchén 来俊臣, had a well-earned reputation for extracting confessions from accused criminals. In fact, once you were put into one of his torture chambers, whether you committed the crime or you were just being falsely accused, everyone confessed.

03:38   Even though she had killed practically everyone who could possibly be a threat to her, Wǔ Zétiān sat uneasily on her throne in historic Luòyáng. There were constant rumors flying around Luòyáng about who was making a move against who. One day someone told someone that they heard from someone that Zhōu Xìng had been in cahoots with the general Qiū Shénjī 丘神勣. General Qiū had been recently executed for plotting against Wǔ Zétiān.

CHINESE SAYINGS BOOK 3
EPISODE 2

04:09 | Empress Wu called Lái Jùnchén to the palace and said she heard Zhōu Xìng was up to something and to go investigate and interrogate.

04:19 | Zhōu Xìng was another secret police official. He worked under Lái Jùnchén and had also developed quite a terrifying reputation for his one hundred per cent conviction record and all his grisly ways of extracting confessions. His reputation was well-earned and there were plenty of stories about all these innocent people who were wrongfully convicted and brutally executed at the hands of Zhōu Xìng.

04:48 | So Lái Jùnchén invited Zhōu Xìng to the palace for a lunch and some vino. Zhōu Xìng and Lái Jùnchén of course knew each other and were already good buds. While they were engaged in their drinking Lái Jùnchén casually said to Zhōu Xìng, "I gotta tell you, man, I've been having the damndest time trying to extract confessions from some of these accused. I try everything and sometimes they still refuse. Zhōu Xìng, people say you're the master. What's your tried and true method for getting people to talk."

05:24 | Zhōu Xìng answered, "The urn. This one never fails. I get a big urn and heat it with white hot coals on four sides. But first, before I light the fires, I stick the accused inside the urn. As soon as it heats up enough, they start screaming out their confessions. Then I execute them."

05:46 | Lái Jùnchén said, "Brilliant. I never thought of that." Then he called out to some of his underlings and

CHINESE SAYINGS BOOK 3
EPISODE 2

demands an urn be brought out and to get a fire going as Zhōu Xìng described.

06:00 Zhōu Xìng was wondering what's going on here. Lái Jùnchén said to him,"Empress Wu heard from one of her peoples that you were conspiring with Qiū Shénjīn against the state." Zhōu Xìng said this is preposterous and just wild comments made by his enemies. He totally denied everything.

06:21 So Lái Jùnchén said to Zhōu Xìng, okay then in that case, please get inside this urn. Qǐng Jūn, invite the gentleman. Rù wèng, enter the urn. Zhōu Xìng knew right away where this was heading. Lái Jùnchén was using Zhōu Xìng's gruesome interrogation methods against him. And now the tables were turned and he was being forced to suffer the same torture he inflicted on others.

06:49 Or as we say, he was getting a taste of his own medicine. Well, Zhōu Xìng threw himself on the ground before Lái Jùnchén and kowtowed furiously, confessing to everything and admitting his guilt. Lái Jùnchén had him remanded over the authorities and dutifully reported his findings to Wǔ Zétiān.

07:13 The empress must have been having a good day because she considered Zhōu Xìng's past loyalty to her and being there at key times as she was clawing her way to the top. So she didn't call for his execution. She banished him instead. So his life was ruined and as he began making his way to his place of exile, leaving the splendid life of Luòyáng behind, word had gotten out, of course. And

CHINESE SAYINGS BOOK 3
EPISODE 2

many of his enemies were lying in wait for him and when they found him, they made fast work of Zhōu Xìng and brutally killed him.

07:48   So Lái Jùnchén was giving Zhōu Xìng a taste of his own medicine by inviting the gentleman into the urn, the same method of torture that Zhōu Xìng often used against those he dealt with, no matter guilty or innocent. So when you say Qǐng Jūn Rù Wèng it means someone is suffering the same grisly fate using the method that he had reserved for someone else. To fall into one's own trap, so to speak.

08:17   Qǐng Jūn Rù Wèng. A classic. Lái Jùnchén by the way, he too got caught up in a scandal and ended up getting executed. If you think people hated Zhōu Xìng, get a load of what they did to Lái Jùnchén. After he met his end, it's said some of his enemies, which he had plenty, ripped apart his body and ate his flesh and ripped out his organs!

08:45   On that note, I will leave you. This is Laszlo Montgomery signing off from sunny and beautiful LA California. Until the next time, mes amis, I hope you'll keep coming back for more great stuff, here at the Chinese Sayings Podcast.

Chinese Sayings Book 3
Episode 3

BETTING THE BANK

孤注一掷—Gū Zhù Yī Zhì

TRANSCRIPT

00:00	Hey everyone welcome to the season one finale of the Chinese Sayings Podcast. Man, that flew by! Episode ten already.
00:10	For the first time, I get to say this chengyu or Chinese Saying isn't from the Zhōu Dynasty. No Spring and Autumn, Warring States or anything like that. We're in the fabulous Sòng Dynasty. The Northern Sòng in all its splendor and glory.
00:30	This is the time of the third Song Dynasty emperor, Zhēnzōng. His father was the younger brother of the Song Dynasty founder Zhào Kuāngyìn. We're still in the good old days as far as the Northern Song is concerned.
00:44	Today, we'll look at the backstory behind the old saying, Gū Zhù Yī Zhì. Here's the blow by blow.
00:53	Gū in this case means alone or solitary.

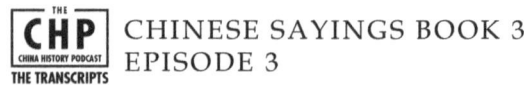

CHINESE SAYINGS BOOK 3
EPISODE 3

00:56 | Zhù has several meanings, but here it means the stakes, as in a gambling wager.

01:04 | Gūzhù, a single wager.

01:07 | Yī is the character for one, the number one.

01:11 | And Zhì means to throw but in this example means to throw dice.

01:17 | Yīzhì, one throw of the dice.

00:20 | A solitary wager, throw the dice. Okay, no need to explain what that means. You bet all your chips on one throw of the dice. Not terribly difficult.

01:29 | So let me call Sherman and Mr. Peabody and let's hop inside the Wayback Machine and head to the time of the late 10th, early 11th Century and let's see what's up with the Zhēnzōng Emperor.

00:41 | Let's introduce today's lineup of stars. I already mentioned the Sòng Emperor Zhēnzōng. There's also his chancellor Kòu Zhǔn 寇准 and the minister Wáng Qīnruò. Those two were not friendly or close.

01:58 | We remember from all those CHP episodes that even though the Sòng Dynasty was a great time in Chinese history commercially, economically, artistically, gastronomically and in a dozen other ways. Despite all that, they were surrounded by enemies. And the cost to defend themselves by maintaining massive six-figure

CHINESE SAYINGS BOOK 3
EPISODE 3

standing armies and to pay off the various northern and western people... that cost was not small.

02:24 Soon after Zhēnzōng became emperor, the great power of that day, the Khitan Liáo Dynasty to the north, decided to test the emperor's mettle. In Mandarin, these people were known as the Qìdān 契丹. During the summer in the year 1004, they invaded from the north and Song forces battled them but couldn't hold them back.

02:47 We featured the Khitan Liáo founder Ābǎojī 阿保机 in an old CHP episode number 126. In their day, they were the biggest and baddest of them all. So in this moment of crisis, with the Liáo forces fast approaching, the emperor was first visited by his minister Wáng Qīnruò who advised him better close down shop and get out of town before the Khitan's get here. He suggested to move the capital, which in those days meant to move the emperor, to where present day Nánjīng is, on the south side of the Yangzi River.

03:22 Another official named Chén Yáosǒu approached Zhēnzōng and suggested maybe it was a better idea to move the capital out to Chéngdū, far from harm's way, where he came from. No one was saying let's stay and fight. Zhēnzōng was really starting to get a bad feeling about everything and went to his most trusted minister Kòu Zhǔn to ask him what he thought. The important thing about Kòu Zhǔn is that in Chinese history when you list out all the top ten chancellors, or prime ministers, he always makes the list. He was one of the good ones.

CHINESE SAYINGS BOOK 3
EPISODE 3

03:59 | Anyways, he got wind of what Wáng Qīnruò and Chén Yáosǒu were advocating and he went before Zhēnzōng and said, pretending not to know who made those two proposals, that abandoning Kāifēng was a terrible idea. And that whoever proposed such a thing, Kòu Zhǔn said, was committing a capital crime.

04:20 | Kòu Zhǔn and his supporters said they should stand and fight. He said so great is his majesty's royal presence, if he showed up to personally rally the Song troops against the Khitan Liao, it would lead them to victory. The chancellor continued saying that the Khitan Army, 200,000 strong had come a long way and were in unfamiliar territory and worn out already. Song forces had several advantages over them. Why walk away from the ancestral temple in Kāifēng so easy? So persuasive was Kòu Zhǔn that Emperor Zhēnzōng followed his advice and he went out to the front to rally the troops against the Khitan Liao army.

05:04 | When he caught up with his army somewhere north of Kāifēng, the soldiers and civilians' spirits were uplifted and indeed the Emperor's royal presence provided the moral support that allowed them to push the Liao back and to defeat them at the town of Chányuān, a hundred miles north of the Song capital. And from this defeat of the Liao came the Treaty of Chányuān, the Chányuān Zhī Méng 澶渊之盟.

05:31 | The Khitan's agreed not to invade Song territory in exchange for a huge chunk of change and for henceforth being treated as diplomatic equals to the

18

CHINESE SAYINGS BOOK 3
EPISODE 3

Emperor in Kaifeng. So they got paid off essentially, but the arrangement worked for twenty years and there was relative peace between Liao and Song. But if you remember from those past China History Podcast episodes, all the other bad guys surrounding China will see what the Khitan's did and then they'll try and cut similar deals with the Song emperor and then the business model became untenable.

06:09 So the emperor went back to Kaifeng triumphant and you can imagine Kòu Zhǔn was the hottest property in the government. He was the one who came up with the idea to take the fight to the Khitan's and he stood by the emperor's side throughout the ordeal. But Wáng Qīnruò never forgave Kòu Zhǔn for challenging him so brazenly in front of the big guy. So he was bent on toppling Kòu Zhǔn.

06:34 One day when he had the emperor's ear he at once began bad-mouthing Kòu Zhǔn and saying this whole Treaty of Chányuān was a shameful moment for the nation. He compared the acquiescence at Chányuān to a similar treaty from ancient times signed under duress, when the enemy was already at the city walls. He really laid into how Kòu Zhǔn just gave away the store.

07:00 Wáng Qīnruò began to see the emperor was wavering now where he stood. So he said to him, Kòu Zhǔn was using the emperor's life as an all-or-nothing wager. He acted like a classic reckless gambler. And in the Book of Kòu Zhǔn from the Sòng Shū, the Book of Song, it said he was accused of Gū Zhù Yī Zhì. And Wáng Qīnruò

CHINESE SAYINGS BOOK 3
EPISODE 3

was able to convince the emperor that his so-called loyal minister Kòu Zhǔn used the emperor as a Gūzhù, like a double-or-nothing wager. Maybe the wager succeeded, but it was a gamble that recklessly used the emperor's royal person.

07:42 So ever since hearing that, Zhēnzōng began to give Kòu Zhǔn the cold shoulder. He didn't banish him or anything, but he did fob him off to a less prestigious posting than the palace at Kaifeng.

07:55 And this chengyu Gū Zhù Yī Zhì has come to describe a reckless gamble. Betting the bank on one throw of the dice. Even though it worked out for the Sòng in their relations with the Khitan Liáo, it was reckless nonetheless.

08:10 And that me little beauties is going to be that. Gū Zhù, a single wager. Yī Zhì one throw of the dice. To bet the bank. Sometimes you win. Sometimes you lose. And sometimes the blues just get a hold of you.

08:27 That's our chengyu for this time, our tenth and final episode for Season One. I'm gonna take a few weeks off, relax in St. Barth's and maybe meet up with Ringo in Monte Carlo. We'll see. Rest assured, Season Two is coming your way soon. But not too soon. You know what they say about all work and no play.

08:47 This is Laszlo Montgomery signing off once again from the City of Angels, California USA. Don't forget there's more than just this Chinese Sayings Podcast. There's the

CHINESE SAYINGS BOOK 3
EPISODE 3

China History Podcast and Tea History Podcast, all from Teacup Media. Go check it out. I'm not asking you to leave a review or a five star rating, but if you want to, I won't hold it against you. Take care everyone!

 Chinese Sayings Book 3
Episode 4

THE TRANSCRIPTS

DOUBLE SORROW

人琴俱亡—Rén Qín Jù Wáng

TRANSCRIPT

00:00	Hi Everyone thanks for coming back. Laszlo Montgomery here again with another Chinese Saying, and a musical one at that.
00:10	Today we're going to look at Rén Qín Jù Wáng 人琴俱亡. Spoiler alert, like last week this one sort of ends on a bit of a downer. And let me say right up front this is a chengyu that you hope you never have to use.
00:23	Rén Qín Jù Wáng. Let's pick it apart.
00:29	Rén is a person or in this case a man.
00:31	Qín, once again we run into this character. A qín in a Chinese lute or zither. Like you recall from the recent episode Duì Niú Tán Qín, play a lute to an ox.
00:44	Jù means all, entirely, together.
00:50	And the character wáng means to die.

23

CHINESE SAYINGS BOOK 3
EPISODE 4

00:54 So Rén Qín Jù Wáng. Person, qin, together, die. Other than the pre-knowledge that this story isn't going to end well it's hard to extract the meaning out of those four syllables. So let's go find the key that unlocks this door.

01:15 The chūzì 出自 or derivation of this Chinese Saying is one we have never used before. It came out during the Nanbei Chao 南北朝, the Southern and Northern Dynasties Period, 420-589. This followed the Eastern Jin 东晋. The work is called the Shìshuō Xīnyǔ 世说新语. This was credited to one Liu Yiqing of the Liu Song, first of the Southern Dynasties. The Shìshuō Xīnyû was a book of anecdotes about all kinds of literati who lived during the preceding Jin Dynasty.

01:50 This story is special—I know I always say that—because the people in it, a father and his two sons were legends in their own time. The father was featured once as the topic of CHP episode 96 which told the story of the life of calligrapher extraordinaire Wáng Xīzhī 王羲之. He lived during the Eastern Jin Dynasty from 321-379 back when the capital was in Jiànkāng 建康, modern day Nanjing.

02:18 I'm not going to say he was the greatest calligrapher of all time, but he's usually the pat answer when anyone asks who was the greatest calligrapher in ancient China. His work the Lántíng Xù 兰亭序 or "Preface to the Poems Collected from the Orchid Pavilion" is a major work from ancient times and was copied by many who followed.

CHINESE SAYINGS BOOK 3
EPISODE 4

02:40 | Wang Xizhi was serving as an official down in Shàoxīng 绍兴 when he did this masterwork. If any originals of the Lanting Xu exist, they're tucked away in someone's private collection. It's said the Taizong emperor, co-founder of the Tang Dynasty, insisted on being buried with an original.

02:59 | So Wang Xizhi is traditionally called China's greatest calligrapher. Greatest or not, he did get the moniker of Shū Shèng 书圣 or the saint of calligraphy. An anonymous buyer in China back in 2010 forked over $46 million for a reproduction of Wang Xīzhī's work done in the Tang. So you might say he's quite respected in the world of Chinese culture and even more so in the world of Chinese calligraphy.

03:31 | Well, after all this hype I regret to say Wang Xizhi isn't actually in our story today. But two of his seven sons were. And many who are expert in calligraphy say the youngest son, Wang Xiànzhī 王献之, was just as good as his saintly father. The older son Huīzhī 王徽之 was also renowned in his day, but to most, Wang Xizhi and Wang Xiànzhī are the two more familiar names.

03:57 | But one day in his prime, Wang Xianzhi passed away suddenly, in his early 40's. When he was alive, he would often relax by playing the qín and he became quite proficient in this instrument. If he ever played it to an ox, I can't say for sure.

04:16 | So when brother Huīzhī attended the funeral of his younger brother and he approached the bier, he didn't

CHINESE SAYINGS BOOK 3
EPISODE 4

shed a tear. He stood before his brother's coffin silently. Next to the coffin lay Wang Xianzhi's qín. And Huizhi reached for it and tried, in vein I might add, to tune it or extract some familiar melody from it. No matter how hard he tried, Huīzhī couldn't get the instrument to yield anything. So with the tears welling up in his eyes, he smashed it to the ground and cried to his dearly departed brother that both his qín or lute had died along with him. Both the man and the lute had perished. And let me close this story by saying Wang Huizhi himself died of a broken heart only a month later.

05:11 The Rén Qín, the man and the lute or zither, Jù both, together, wáng, died.

05:18 Rén Qín Jù Wáng. The sad story of the brothers Wang, sons of one China's greatest men of letters, Wang Xizhi. CHP episode 96 if you want to hear a little more about the Shū Shèng, the calligraphy saint, and the times he lived in. He was one of the many literary greats to come out of that most literary of cities, Shàoxīng in Zhèjiāng Province.

05:46 So, as I said, this is a chengyu we all hope we never have to use. But in cases where you see some memento or other that brings back memories of a dear one who in life possessed the object, this chengyu Rén Qín Jù Wáng is an expression of that great sadness and grief you might feel when you see something that reminds you of your loss.

CHINESE SAYINGS BOOK 3
EPISODE 4

06:15 | So that's the skinny on that one. Sorry I can't drag this out anymore than I did. I think perhaps this was more of a brief history lesson on Wang Xizhi than anything else. Anyway I hope you enjoyed this nice musical chengyu.

06:30 | Rén Qín Jù Wáng. The man and the qín, both have perished.

06:36 | Okay, without further ado or any commercials or needless filler material, let's call it a day right here and now. This is Laszlo Montgomery, yeah, I know, same guy as the China History Podcast and China Vintage Hour. All part of the sprawling Teacup Media empire. Go check all that stuff out at the usual places and of course Teacup.media.

06:59 | Okay, see you next time everyone. At least I hope so. I'll have yet another nice musical chengyu for your ever-growing collection. Take care all.

 Chinese Sayings Book 3
Episode 5

WHOLE LOTTA LOVE

琴瑟和鸣—Qín Sè Hè Míng

TRANSCRIPT

00:00 | Welcome back, ladies and gentlemans, Laszlo Montgomery here with one more halfway decent and interesting Chinese Saying, the penultimate of this second season. This chengyu's a little more upbeat than the last two, but not without its share of tragedy.

00:18 | We don't go back too far in this episode, relatively speaking that is. We're only at the dismal conclusion of the Northern Song and its aftermath down in Hangzhou. Most of our chengyu's are rooted in the Eastern Zhou Dynasty, Spring & Autumn and Warring States periods. But not this one. It took place a good 1,500 years after those feudalistic times.

00:43 | Today we're going to look at Qín Sè Hè Míng 琴瑟和鸣. Not sure if any of you have heard that one before. Doesn't make it to any top ten lists as far as I know.

00:54 | Qín Sè Hè Míng. Let's do what we always do.

CHINESE SAYINGS BOOK 3
EPISODE 5

00:59 Qín, yeah the same qín as Duì Niú Tán Qín 对牛弹琴. Play a lute to an ox and Rén Qín Jù Wáng 人琴俱亡, both man and lute have perished. Qín can be a general term for a stringed instrument, but today is always referred to as a seven stringed gǔqín 古琴.

01:16 And then here's another new instrument for you called a Sè. This is a bigger instrument with anywhere from 25-50 strings. This musical instrument went all the way back to the Zhou dynasty so it's as ancient as the gǔqín.

01:31 So, Qín Sè. The Qín and the Sè. Then there's hè 和 just like from the previous episode Qǔ Gāo Hè Guǎ 曲高和寡 if the tune is too highfalutin, ain't no one gonna sing it (although I don't think my chengyu zidian put it quite that way.) In the fourth tone, that character means to join in the singing or to chime in with others.

01:54 And last character míng, we've come across this one before. Remember from season one Jī Míng Gou Dào 鸡鸣狗盗, crow like a cock and snatch like a dog. To use low-handed tricks to get what you want. Same Míng. It means of birds, insects and mammals to cry out, to crow. But in our case today, it means more like to sing or make a sound.

02:16 Qín Sè Hè Míng. The Qin and the Se sing along sound. Not terribly revealing is it?

02:24 So you know what that means. We're left with no choice except to dig below the surface to uncover the story from whence this chengyu sprang. And once this story is told,

CHINESE SAYINGS BOOK 3
EPISODE 5

these four characters that appear randomly selected out of a hat all the sudden make perfect sense.

02:41 The story, as I said, took place during some of the darkest hours of the Song Dynasty. These years during the 1120's were covered in the previous China History Podcast episode 23 on the Song Dynasty and then again in more gory detail in that four-part series on the Huizong Emperor.

03:01 Although our story takes place during the Song, the source of the material came from a Yuán Dynasty collection of poems called the Ài Lán Xuān 爱兰轩. Couldn't dig up too much on that.

03:12 The two main characters of today's story were far from a couple of nobodies. Zhào Míngchéng 赵明诚 and Li Qīngzhào 李清照. Zhào Míngchéng lived from 1081 to 1129 and was a giant in the field of Ancient Chinese epigraphy. Yeah, I know, what's that. Epigraphy is the study of ancient inscriptions. Words and symbols that are carved into substrates like stone or metal. He also was quite accomplished in the arts and letters and came from a respectable lineage that today coulda got him a ground floor table at the Luk Yu Teahouse in Hong Kong.

03:47 Li Qīngzhào is ranked as among the greatest female poets in all of Chinese history. And let me say, that's quite a claim to fame. You had to be pretty darn good to share that superlative. She lived 1084-1155. So you can see she lived twenty-six years longer than Zhào Míngchéng.

04:10 | They were both from Shandong province. Li Qīngzhào also had quite a background. Her father had studied under no less a superstar than Sū Dōngpō, Sū Shì, who we featured in a standalone episode CHP-175. Her father was an amazing scholar and like many a Song era literatus, he had a pretty decent library. And Li Qīngzhào grew up amongst all these books and soaked up all she could from them. She was incredible and already in her teens it was said she was very much admired for her poetry. She was quite a favorite in the more elite circles of aristocrats.

04:49 | The two met. Zhao was 20 and Li was 18. In 1101 they married and to call this a match made in heaven would be the understatement of the century. These two were in love and devoted to each other like you cannot believe. And to top it all off, as if this true love they had for each other wasn't enough, they both shared this passion for epigraphy and would scour the markets together looking for any inscriptions that they could study together and add to their museum quality collection. Sometimes Zhào Míngchéng would arrive home wearing almost nothing because it was not unusual for him to pawn the clothes on his back in order to acquire some piece or another that he saw in some antiques market.

05:43 | When Zhào Míngchéng received his degree and began his career as an official in the Northern Song bureaucracy, he wasn't making much money. But even in their relative poverty you couldn't find a happier couple. When they were together they would sit side by side and decipher these old inscriptions. They'd practice

CHINESE SAYINGS BOOK 3
EPISODE 5

calligraphy together, paint, engage in witty repartee and sing couplets to each other, replying to the other in the most elegant and poetic ways. Oh man, they had a blast together. So in love, the preacher's face turned red.

06:15 Together they collaborated on the work that Zhào Míngchéng is most remembered for, the Jīnshí Lù 金石录 a 30-volume work that was revered as the greatest academic milestone in Chinese epigraphy going back to the Shāng Dynasty.

06:33 So this happy couple lived in sheer and utter conjugal bliss for many years. And then in the 1120's trouble came from the north. The Jürchens, who later on would be known as the Manchu's, flooded out of their lands in Manchuria and put an end to what became known as the Northern Song Dynasty. By 1127 it was all over and the magnificent Song capital city of Kaifeng was reduced to cinders and the entire royal family was sent packing to the coldest most desolate parts of Heilongjiang to live out the rest of their lives.

07:10 And Zhao Mingcheng and Li Qīngzhào, they fled south, first to Nanjing. One Song Dynasty royal had gotten away and reconstituted the dynasty down in present day Hangzhou and so began the Southern Song. Like so many other northerners who fled for their lives in terror, Zhao Mingcheng and Li Qīngzhào had to sort of start their lives all over. Like other ethnic minorities who are forced to flee in the middle of the night, they could only cart away a limited amount of their vast possessions, including their collection. And in their haste to put as many tracks as possible between them and the Jürchens, they had to dump plenty of stuff along the way. Whatever was left behind, so lovingly and painstakingly sorted, studied and cared for, was destroyed by the Jürchens.

08:03 Though the happy couple survived that national trauma, Zhao Mingcheng didn't bounce from the Jürchen invasion and he died in 1129. He left behind his unfinished work, the Jīnshí Lù as well as all the research that still needed to be done with all the couple's various epigraphic pursuits.

08:25 Li Qīngzhào was heartbroken. Her beloved husband Zhao Mingcheng was gone, the man who had always been an inspiration for many of her greatest poems. He had been more than a soul mate and losing him so young punched a giant hole in her life.

08:44 What could she do except keep on keeping on. She moved to Hangzhou, one of China's great centers of the arts and letters. She continued to produce her poetry. She helped to finish off the Jīnshí Lù, lived plainly, and till her dying day honored and cherished the memory of her husband Zhao Mingcheng. She had experienced a rollercoaster life filled with greatest happiness and most miserable despair. Anyone who lived through the Jürchen invasion didn't have it easy, if they survived at all. It was a shocking upheaval and ended up being only a dress rehearsal for the Mongol invasion a hundred forty years later.

CHINESE SAYINGS BOOK 3
EPISODE 5

09:27 So you can now see the meaning of this idiom Qín Sè Hè Míng. The two instruments Qín Sè represent Zhao Mingcheng and Li Qingzhao. Hè Míng singing songs back and forth. Qín Sè Hè Míng. That describes a perfect relationship, especially a marriage. Perfect harmony and conjugal bliss. Qín Sè Hè Míng. If you can say this about the relationship you're in now, then gongxi ni 恭喜你, mazel tov, and congratulations. What can be better than that? Li Qingzhao, this great poet, about sixty to a hundred of her poems managed to make it to our day. As I said, like Muhammed Ali, people called her the greatest.

10:16 Okay, Laszlo Montgomery signing off for a ninth time this musical season. You know where I'm recording this. It isn't a professional recording studio, I'm sure you can tell that. There's more where this came from. So please, please me and do come back next time for another nice tasty chengyu here at the Chinese Sayings Podcast.

Chinese Sayings Book 3
Episode 6

CREATE YOUR DESTINY

乘风破浪—Chéng Fēng Pò Làng

TRANSCRIPT

00:00	Hey everyone welcome back. Laszlo Montgomery here as promised, seven days later. Back with another Chinese Saying. If you're not looking for the Chinese Sayings Podcast then you're on the wrong flight.
00:14	Today's a good one. We can all use this one every now and then. We look at a nice useful chengyu from a period we don't visit that often, the Nán Bei Cháo 南北朝, the Southern and Northern Dynasties Period 386 to 589, basically from the end of the Jìn 晋朝 to the start of the Suí 隋朝. China, temporarily, not a unified nation.
00:37	Wow, feels nice to get away from the Zhōu and Hàn for once. Today we look at Chéng Fēng Pò Làng 乘风破浪. Let's break it apart and see what it means, shall we?
00:46	Chéng Fēng Pò Làng.
00:49	First character Chéng means to ride, like ride a bus, ride an aircraft.

 CHINESE SAYINGS BOOK 3
EPISODE 6

00:54 | Second character Fēng means the wind. Chéngfēng. Ride the wind.

01:00 | Pò in this case, you know, one of those characters with more than the usual amount of definitions. Here it means to break, split, to cleave in two or cut.

01:11 | And Làng is a wave, like an ocean wave. So Pò Làng means to cut through the waves.

01:18 | Chéng Fēng Pò Làng. Ride Wind Cut Waves or cut through the waves, let's say. That could mean anything.

01:27 | Coming to us courtesy of the Sòng Shū 宋书, the Book of Song, is this story, as I said, from Southern and Northern Dynasties period. This story takes place during the time of the Liú Sòng Dynasty 刘宋超, one of the Southern Dynasties, their capital at Jiànkāng, today known as the city of Nánjīng. This was discussed in the China History Podcast episode number 23. The Sòng Shū refers to this dynasty, not the Song dynasty situated between the Yuan 元朝 and Ming 明朝 on the China history timeline.

02:00 | There was this young kid named Zōng Què 宗悫. And he was fearless. He had practiced martial arts practically since birth with his father and his uncle, the younger brother of his father. Both men were very skilled and taught Zōng Què how to handle a sword, how to stand your ground and how to fight.

02:19 | And he grew up, this young lad, blending in easily with the timeless landscape around present day Dèngzhōu

38

CHINESE SAYINGS BOOK 3
EPISODE 6

邓州, Hénán province, where he lived, doing the same chores as everyone around him who came before, and no doubt after too. But as he carried out all his duties, filial and otherwise, in his young head he had great dreams and would see himself as this warrior, celebrated for his bravery.

02:50 | When he was fourteen, his brother got married. Back in those days, bandits roamed the countryside, often terrorizing peasants and robbing them of whatever meager possessions they had. And they fell on Zōng Què's family on the day of the wedding, about a dozen of them, and started pushing people around, acting tough and making all kinds of demands for everyone to surrender their valuables.

03:18 | Well, remember that unforgettable scene in Billy Jack, the 1971 classic film? That's what Zōng Què did. He sprang into action and using all the martial arts skills acquired from his father and his uncle throughout the years, he beat the living daylights out of these banditos. And he sent them packing, some of them were wounded badly.

03:41 | Well, you can imagine how everyone felt after seeing that young fourteen year old Zōng Què daring to stand up to such strength and numbers. And defeating them. His uncle saw everything and asked Zōng Què one day what was his destiny. What did he want to do with his life. And as it's written in the Book of Song, Zong Que replied, "Yuàn chéng cháng fēng. Pò wànlǐ làng. Gàn yī fān wěidà de shìyè. 愿乘长风破万里浪,干一番伟大的事业. He wanted to ride the wind and crash through the

CHINESE SAYINGS BOOK 3
EPISODE 6

waves and build a great career. So, tucked inside those sixteen characters are the words, Chéng Fēng Pò Làng, ride the wind, Chéngfēng 乘风 and break or cut through the waves 破浪.

04:29 And I'll tell you, Zōng Què was true to his word. He wasn't what you'd call a major, or even a minor, character in Chinese history. But he indeed lived during the period of the Liu Song, dying in the year 465. And while the Liu Song was having its time on the stage of Chinese history, Zōng Què served as a military officer known for his bravery and courageousness, particularly his service down in Champa, south of the border, back when this part of present-day Vietnam was still called Línyì 临邑.

04:59 So that's the story of Zōng Què, who was raised by the menfolk in his life to be a skilled fighter. And he put these skills to use first in the defense of his family and later on in the service of his country. When he was young he vowed he would Chéngfēng Pòlàng, ride the wind and cleave through the waves, meaning he would strive to ride high and do whatever it took to succeed.

05:24 So I hope you don't feel short-changed. This story is slightly shorter than the usual chengyu you're used to. But this one is sort of succinct and to the point. Not even Laszlo Montgomery, so many memorable moments of verbosity over the years, can stretch this out any further than this.

CHINESE SAYINGS BOOK 3
EPISODE 6

05:44 | Chéng Fēng Pò Làng. Ride the wind and crash through the waves. He had lofty ambitions and feared no danger or difficulty. Like a fresh grad out of college. Make this one of your mottos. An alternative to Carpe Diem perhaps.

05:59 | So that is going to that for this time. Don't despair you haven't heard the last of me yet. We still have two more episodes to go in this heroic Season 3. I'll be back next week with the penultimate episode. I have another good chengyu lined up for you. I'm going to trot out one of the true sacred cows in ancient Chinese history for episode nine so when I say you ain't gonna want to miss this one, I mean it.

06:29 | Laszlo Montgomery here wishing you all my very best, as always, on behalf of the whole team here at CHP headquarters, a mere hop skip and a jump from the San Andreas Fault. So, barring that geological sword of Damocles slipping any more than its usual 35 mm per year, I'll see you next time for another good one here at the Chinese Sayings Podcast.

Chinese Sayings Book 3
Episode 7

TWO FACED BACK STABBER

口蜜腹剑—Kǒu Mì Fù Jiàn

TRANSCRIPT

00:00	Welcome back again, Laszlo Montgomery here. Another good and decent chéngyǔ for your collection. Another classic, worthy of any self-respecting compendium of Chinese Idioms.
00:11	Kǒu Mì Fù Jiàn 口蜜腹剑, a classic going back to the Zīzhì Tōngjiàn 资治通鉴 presented to the Northern Song Emperor Yīngzōng 宋英宗 in 1084 by one of the great literati of an age of great literati, Sīmǎ Guāng 司马光.
00:25	Besides being a veritable depository of great Chinese Idioms, this classic from Chinese literature usually called "Historical Events Retold as a Mirror for Government" was a history of China from 403 to 959. The start of the Sixteen Kingdoms to the fall of the Later Zhou 北周 and the unification of the north and south of the country by Zhào Kuangyin 赵匡胤 who founded the Song in 960.
00:51	And from this great document, one of the classics from these official histories commissioned by emperors

CHINESE SAYINGS BOOK 3
EPISODE 7

through the dynasties, we get a whole slew of halfway decent chéngyǔ's.

01:02 Including this one, Kǒu Mì Fù Jiàn. A Mouth of Honey and a dagger in the belly.

01:09 These four characters, kǒu is a mouth.

01:13 Mì is honey.

01:15 Fù is your belly, abdomen or stomach.

01:19 And a Jiàn is a double edged sword.

01:22 Mouth Honey Stomach or belly Sword. This is one of those that could be anything. You need to know the back story.

01:30 This one goes back to the Tang Dynasty, the time of Emperor Xuánzōng whose Kāiyuán Era 开元年号 was a golden age during this dynasty. The villain in the story is his chancellor for eighteen years, Lǐ Línfú 李林甫. He dominated the Tang government during his long run as chancellor and Xuánzōng trusted him with his life.

01:56 The thing about Lǐ Línfú was that he was known for the way he would flatter you to your face. And the way he went on and on with Emperor Xuánzōng, it was the stuff of legends. He would butter up the emperor like nothing else and knew how to always stay in Xuánzōng's good graces.

CHINESE SAYINGS BOOK 3
EPISODE 7

02:15 | And not only to the emperor. Even to everyone else at court. To their face he would be nothing except the most genteel, self-effacing, respectful, complimentary person you can imagine, even being such a high-ranking person in the government, right hand man to the emperor. He couldn't say enough good things to his fellow officials to their face when he saw them.

02:39 | But one thing about Lǐ Línfú, he was a very jealous and paranoid guy and had a compulsive fear that someone else at court might outshine him and replace him. So whenever the emperor would ask him about promoting so and so, Lǐ Línfú would assure the emperor, bad choice. And he would say a few words to disparage the integrity of the man and that was that. Xuánzōng would perish the thought.

03:06 | And that guy, who Lǐ Línfú stabbed in the back, that same morning the chancellor just couldn't have been more commendatory, praising him up and down. And applauding his daily work. But when it came time to put in a good word for him to the emperor, he stabbed him in the back and gave false accusations.

03:24 | And Lǐ Línfú was notorious for this. And for years and years, good and capable officials were denied promotions or to serve in positions of power because Lǐ Línfú didn't want anyone getting a leg up on him or even get close to the emperor who he manipulated with flattery and through a network of spies that informed him of every single conversation, encounter, whisper and secret that went on in the nèitíng 内廷, the inner palace where the

CHINESE SAYINGS BOOK 3
EPISODE 7

emperor lived.

03:57 And what ended up happening over time was that with so many capable officials denied key positions in government, what the emperor got instead was a lot of mediocrity and ho-hum ministers who were beholden to Lǐ Línfú.

04:13 And without proper stewardship of this greatest empire that China had ever seen in its history, things indeed deteriorated. Lǐ Línfú died in 753 and within a few years the whole dynasty was in danger of being torn down by the devastation of the Ān Lùshān Rebellion of 755 to 763.

04:36 So this one is useful. People today are by nature still the same as they were in the 8th Century. And the classic two-faced back-stabber who is so pleasant and nice to you when you're face to face with them, but destroys you when he talks to others about you behind your back. Never goes out of style. And maybe some of you have had the misfortune to be acquainted with one or two of these types.

04:59 Their mouth is honey, Kǒu mì 口蜜. But in their belly lies a sword, fù jiàn 腹剑.

05:06 Kǒu Mì Fù Jiàn. Pleco defines this Chinese Saying as "honey-mouthed and dagger hearted; hypocritical and malignant; with an iron hand in a velvet glove; a Judas kiss. Hypocritical and murderous."

CHINESE SAYINGS BOOK 3
EPISODE 7

05:22 Stay away from these types. With their gloved tie and firm handshake, sudden look in the eye and their easy smile.

05:0 Lǐ Línfú, by the way, he got his in the end. After he died, someone went to Xuánzōng and just dumped on him, accused Lǐ Línfú of all these terrible things he did to cause trouble for the emperor. And because of this, after giving Lǐ Línfú a funeral fit for a king with all kinds of posthumous honors, he had him stripped of everything and given a commoners funeral and grave. And for good measure, because this was one of things they used to do back in those days, they exiled his whole family to a place much less pleasant to live than the capital Cháng'ān.

06:06 So if you know someone, at work, at the gym, amongst your groups of friends and colleagues, and one of them is always nice to you but you suspect they are trashing you when you ain't around, they are Kǒu Mì Fù Jiàn.

06:21 Be careful around these Kǒu Mì Fù Jiàn people in person and online!

06:27 Okay, that's today's Chinese Saying. This is a very well known chéngyǔ. But like it is with a lot of these Chinese Idioms, there's always some story that goes with it. And that, mes amis, is the whole raison d'être of the Chinese Sayings Podcast. All right, that's all I have for you today.

06:44 Don't forget, besides this fine program suitable for people of all ages, there's also the Tea History Podcast and the

CHINESE SAYINGS BOOK 3
EPISODE 7

flagship program of the whole Teacup Media Network, the China History Podcast. Find those fine programs wherever podcasts are given away free. You can also find them at the website at teacup.media. Everything is there all in one place, along with downloadable pdf's of all the Chinese terms used in the episode.

07:14 Okay, Laszlo Montgomery signing off from Los Angeles in beautiful Southern California. Take care and come back again next time for another golden nugget here at the Chinese Sayings Podcast.

Chinese Sayings Book 3 Episode 8

A FARCICAL ENDING

狗尾續貂—Gǒu Wěi Xù Diāo

TRANSCRIPT

00:00 | Greetings one and all. So happy you decided to return for one more priceless gem from the annals of Chinese history, a history that has provided us with so many wonderful chéngyǔ's, like this one: Gǒu Wěi Xù Diāo狗尾续貂.

00:18 | Now this story may take a while to tell because it comes from one of the wildest, craziest and bloodiest periods in early Chinese history, the late 3rd and early 4th centuries. What a raucous time that was. If you recall, the Qín Dynasty fell in 209 BCE followed by the Hàn 209 BCE to 220 CE, then The Three Kingdoms 220-280.

00:46 | Our chengyu for this time comes from that period that stretched from the final years of the Three Kingdoms to the end of the Western Jìn. The stars of this tale are of course the Sīmǎ 司马 Clan who dominated this period. And we have the Sīmǎ's stooping to their lowest level in their colorful family history who we must thank for today's offering: Gǒu Wěi Xù Diāo.

CHINESE SAYINGS BOOK 3
EPISODE 8

01:13 | As for the four characters that make up today's chengyu. A gǒu 狗 is a dog and a wěi 尾 is a tail.

01:19 | Gǒuwěi 狗尾, the tail of a dog, a dog's tail.

01:23 | Xù means to continue or join or add to.

01:27 | And a Diāo is a sable, a kind of a marten. Their fur has always been prized, especially in China amongst the emperor and those highest-ranking officials who advised him personally. Some of these officials would wear these elaborate hats, made from sable that had the tail of the animal hanging along the side. They were quite striking.

01:50 | So, this is one of those chengyu's where there's absolutely no way for you to guess what it means just by listening to these four characters, Dog-Tail-Join-Sable.

02:02 | So let's dive right in to this sliver of Chinese history that, in the end, turned out to be so consequential as far as all the things that happened when it was all over.

02:13 | This story has a cast of thousands. So I'm going to advise you to refer to the handy list of terms that I painstakingly compile for you for each and every episode no matter the CHP, THP or CSP. I'll have the whole cast of characters listed there and you can keep all the Sīmǎ's, Yang's, Cáo's and everyone else straight.

02:35 | If you recall your Three Kingdoms history, there was a loyal general and official to none other than Cáo Cáo

50

CHINESE SAYINGS BOOK 3
EPISODE 8

曹操 himself named Sīmǎ Yì 司马懿 who also served subsequent Cáo Wèi 曹魏 emperors. Then came the year 249 when he utilized his power as regent to seize power in Cáo Wèi and essentially ruled the kingdom as a warlord. Then in 266, his grandson Sīmǎ Yán 司马炎 forced the last Cáo Wèi emperor, Cáo Huàn 曹奂, to abdicate. And we remember Sīmǎ Yán today as the founding emperor of the Jìn Dynasty 晋朝, and the founding emperor Jìn Wǔdì 晋武帝.

03:14 Now, one of the first things Sīmǎ Yan did when he sat himself on the throne in Luòyáng was to enfeoff a whole bunch of family members as princes and dukes. The rationale being that they would surround him like a big layer of fat that would insulate him from any treachery sent in his direction by possible contenders. And depending on the rank he handed out, these enfeoffed family members from the Sīmǎ clan had anywhere from five hundred to five thousand soldiers. So right away knowing what we know, this is a recipe for disaster but Jìn Wǔdì never lived to see it. And after he passed in 290, the Jìn Dynasty fortunes will be impacted immediately.

04:01 After a lot of cloak and dagger wrapped up in a web of deception concerning the heir to the throne, Sīmǎ Yán's mentally disabled son, Sīmǎ Zhōng 司马衷, became emperor. No mention of his specific mental affliction, but it was strongly inferred it was sufficiently debilitating whereby he had no business being the ruler of a country.

04:23 But Jìn Emperor Wǔ's wife, the Empress Dowager Yáng held the reins of power from behind the throne. And to

CHINESE SAYINGS BOOK 3
EPISODE 8

back her up, she was allied with her father, the former emperor's longtime ally, Yáng Jùn 杨骏. And both of them spoke up for her son, Sīmǎ Zhōng, who was now the Emperor Huì 晋惠帝.

04:44 But Emperor Hui's wife, the empress, she was a major force of nature and gave good old Empress Dowager Lǚ, Lǚ Hòu 吕后, Hàn Gāozǔ's wife, a run for her money in the villainous and malevolent department. She was not happy at all with the emperor's mother and illustrious grandfather lording it over them and she began to conspire at once how to get rid of those two.

05:11 Empress Dowager Yáng went and did what anyone in her position would do. She filled the imperial court and the government with Yáng family relatives.

05:21 So this wife of Jìn Emperor Huì, named Jiǎ Nánfēng 贾南风, Empress Jiǎ, in her determination to grab hold of the reins of power, conspired with a member of the Sīmǎ clan, namely Sīmǎ Wěi 司马玮, brother to the emperor.

05:35 These two came up with a plan to do away with Empress Dowager Yang and her father. The scheme called for Sīmǎ Wěi to lead his troops into the capital in Luòyáng and Empress Jiǎ would sit on her hands and let this provocative act to happen. Once Sīmǎ Wěi and his troops were in place, Empress Jiǎ had Empress Dowager Yáng and her father Yáng Jùn summarily arrested. An edict was drawn up accusing them both of treason. Whereupon Yáng Jùn was executed and the Empress Dowager Yáng was locked away in a dungeon where

CHINESE SAYINGS BOOK 3
EPISODE 8

she was starved to death.

06:14 Mind you, this is all coming from the Book of Jìn which wasn't compiled till 648, more than three centuries after the events took place. But in all these histories from so long ago, these official annals compiled by court historians, well, that's all we have to hang our hat on for better or for worse.

06:34 And whenever something of this nature goes down, that is, a coup d'état, it's common to go after all the family members of the recently deposed. So Empress Jiǎ gave the okay to execute three thousand or so Yáng family members in positions of authority around the empire. So the team of Sīmǎ Wěi and the Empress Jiǎ made fast work of their rival and now the Empress was able to control the destiny of China beginning in 291.

07:02 Once she felt secure behind the throne Empress Jiǎ called on two old stalwarts of the Sīmǎ's, Wèi Guàn 卫瓘 and Sīmǎ Liàng to act as regents for Emperor Huì. Sīmǎ Liàng was the fourth son of Sīmǎ Yì and grand uncle to the Emperor Huì. Both he and Wèi Guàn ruled as co-regents and a sincere effort was made to do a good job. But Empress Jiǎ would see none of that. She believed she was the ultimate authority for all matters regarding the Sīmǎ Jìn Dynasty. And she interfered with the every decision these two made.

07:40 Soon she began to conspire again with Emperor Huì's brother Sīmǎ Wěi to help her get rid of Wèi Guàn and Sīmǎ Liàng. Sīmǎ Wěi and Empress Jiǎ had formal charges presented that claimed these two regents were conspiring against Emperor Huì. And they moved swiftly to execute the loyal co-regents Sīmǎ Liàng and Wèi Guàn.

08:04 The blood was all on Sīmǎ Wěi's hands and he believed, for doing her bidding the Empress Jiǎ, she'd give him a promotion or something. But rather than a nice pat on the back, she stabbed him in the back instead and in the summer of 291, Year of the Dog appropriately enough, she had Sīmǎ Wěi executed for the execution of Wèi Guàn and Sīmǎ Liàng, something Sīmǎ Wěi had done for the empress herself.

08:33 So Two-Faced Empress Jiǎ got to finally manage the affairs of the Empire unopposed until the year 299. And one thing that dogged her, so to speak, was that she had not been able to sire any sons with her mentally incapacitated husband, Emperor Huì. But one of his concubines had that good fortune and this lad's name was Sīmǎ Yù 司马遹. And Empress Jiǎ didn't like him for obvious reasons and sought to eliminate him.

09:02 She managed to place this young prince, Sīmǎ Yù under house arrest. Now enter Sīmǎ Lún 司马伦, the youngest son of Sīmǎ Yì. Sīmǎ Lún was part of Empress Jiǎ's loyal coterie of supporters. He and Empress Jiǎ put their heads together and he convinced her the best course of action was to have the crown prince Sīmǎ Yù killed. She liked that plan and signed off on it. And in the year 300, Sīmǎ Yù was indeed killed.

CHINESE SAYINGS BOOK 3
EPISODE 8

09:34 | But Sīmǎ Lún, being a rather evil guy himself, he was able to turn the tables on Empress Jiǎ and had her role in all this exposed and she ended up getting arrested and had to pay for her crime by drinking poison. And for good measure, like it always was in these cases, Sīmǎ Lún had Empress Jiǎ's family wiped out.

09:57 | So now with her out of the way, and no one to protect the enfeebled emperor, Sīmǎ Lún declared himself the grand chancellor who ruled for the incapacitated Emperor Huì. With aspirations of greatness in mind, Sīmǎ Lún made the fateful decision in 301 to put the Emperor Huì under house arrest and he promptly declared himself the new emperor.

10:24 | The outrage all over the capital was beyond belief. It sent shock waves throughout the empire, particularly within the Sīmǎ clan. Three Sīmǎ's, Sīmǎ Jiǒng 司马囧, Sīmǎ Yóng 司马颙 and Sīmǎ Yǐng 司马颖, joined together to lead the fight against Sīmǎ Lún who had dared to follow in the footsteps of Wáng Mǎng 王莽 back in 9 CE in usurping the emperorship.

10:52 | Sīmǎ Lún knew from the very start that his claim to the throne was tenuous at best. Ever since he had deposed Empress Jiǎ, he at once tried to get everyone on his side. So before he made this power grab for the emperorship he started passing out titles left and right, hundreds of them in every direction, even thousands.

11:14 | So, from February 3 to May 30 in the year 301, Sīmǎ Lún got to be the emperor. And when it was all over he was

CHINESE SAYINGS BOOK 3
EPISODE 8

arrested by the opposition and promptly executed as well as all his sons too. As for the deposed Emperor Huì, he was retrieved from his house arrest and plopped back on the throne and got to begin a second run as emperor.

11:39 It's written that Sīmǎ Lún, he wasn't the sharpest knife in the drawer and was merely a pawn being controlled by other Sīmǎ's or princes. But thanks to his power grab we ended up with this chéngyǔ: Gǒu Wěi Xù Diāo because so many titles were handed out by Sīmǎ Lún in the run-up to his power grab, they ran out of sable fur to use for the hats that these high-ups wore as a sign of their office.

12:09 So many were the officials appointed by Sīmǎ Lún and so few was the supply of sable fur, well, let me just quote from the Book of Jìn from the chapter Zhào Wáng Lún Zhuàn 赵王伦转, "Every lowly servant and foot-soldier was given an official position. At the imperial morning assemblies, sable trimmed official hats filled the room, and the common people created a saying to satirize the situation: 'There isn't enough sable fur to go around — some of them have to use dog tails instead.'"

12:42 So it's from this saying, Diāo Bùzú, Gǒu Wěi Xù 貂不足狗尾续, that we get this chéngyǔ Gǒu Wěi Xù Diāo. It's used in a derogatory sense to describe a court with too many officials. But it also came to be used in situations where a good first outing was followed up poorly by delivering nothing special. It's used as an idiom to describe a poor follow-up to what at first was considered highly prestigious and well-received, usually in the literary sense. Like, her first book was just incredible.

CHINESE SAYINGS BOOK 3
EPISODE 8

But the second one was awful. Gǒu Wěi Xù Diāo. Same thing can be said about lousy movie sequels.

13:24 You know for the sake of keeping this from spinning out of control, I left out three quarters of the details. I'm telling you, the Western Jìn and the Qín dynasty, as soon as the founder died, it's like the dynasty fell off the edge of the table. The Western Jìn ended up lasting for quite a bit longer than the Qín, but by 311 it was over for the Sīmǎ's and their Western Jìn.

13:49 This period in Chinese history that lasted from 291 to 306 is known as the War of the Eight Princes. Founding Emperor Wǔ, a.k.a. Sīmǎ Yán, he thought he was doing the right thing setting up all his family members with their own personal armies. But that backfired as soon as he died and they spent the next fifteen years trying to kill each other. So intense was the internecine warring, these Sīmǎ princes went so far as to make all these alliances with several non-Han tribes from north of China's borders.

14:25 These rough people from the Mongolian steppe and Ordos region were remembered as the Five Barbarians, the Wǔ Hú 五胡. And so violent and murderous was their takeover of northern China after the fall of the Western Jìn, it caused a mass migration of northern Chinese to the safety of southern China, south of the Yángzǐ River. Among those who kept running all the way to southernmost China were the Hakka people who retained their traditional northern language and culture in Guangdong, Fujian, Jiangxi, Guangxi, and elsewhere.

CHINESE SAYINGS BOOK 3
EPISODE 8

15:02 So Gǒu Wěi Xù Diāo. When you have too many officials in positions and not enough work to go around, Gǒu Wěi Xù Diāo. When a rock star comes out with a great record and follows that up with a bomb, Gǒu Wěi Xù Diāo. Anything that's a poor substitution or replacement for a formerly highly regarded work, Gǒu Wěi Xù Diāo.

15:26 Okay, such a complicated story as this one, it's no wonder we had to go so deep into extra time to tell it. The end of the Three Kingdoms to the end of the War of the Eight Princes in the Western Jìn, what a crazy half century that was.

15:41 Okay, that's your chengyu for this time. I already have a good one all queued up for next time. You won't want to miss that one. I wouldn't. This is Laszlo Montgomery signing off from Los Angeles in l'état d'or inviting you to come back next time for another entertaining and informative episode of the Chinese Sayings Podcast.

**Chinese Sayings Book 3
Episode 9**

THE WOOD MAN

木人石心—Mù Rén Shí Xīn

TRANSCRIPT

00:00 | Hi Everyone Laszlo Montgomery here with another chengyu, another Chinese Saying for votre collection croissante.

00:11 | Another good one for you today. A heroic one I might add. This story like most of these Chinese Sayings harkens back to ancient times. But not as ancient as we're used to. Today we only go back as far as the Western Jin Dynasty when they had their capital first at Luòyáng and for the last few years in Cháng'ān.

00:31 | The Sīmǎ's of the Jìn weren't the first ones to govern from those two most ancient capitals of China and they weren't the last. The Western Jin lasted from 265 to 316 CE, falling hard around the time of the Great Constantine I in Rome. These were the good old days for the Jìn. But this dynasty didn't last long unfortunately.

CHINESE SAYINGS BOOK 3
EPISODE 9

00:54   You remember from all those past China History Podcast episodes that once the Western Jìn fell in 316, China faced about two and a half centuries of disunity before Yáng Jiān 杨坚 unified the lands in 581 and founded the Suí Dynasty..

01:10   Our Chéngyǔ for this time comes to us courtesy of the Jìn Shū 晋书 The Book of Jìn, compiled during the early Tang Dynasty during the reign of the great Tàizōng Emperor 唐太宗. You'll find this chengyu mentioned in the 49th scroll in the chapter Yǐnyìliè Zhuàn 隐逸列传.

01:28   And the first of the two stars of our chengyu story was a crony of the Sīmǎ's named Jiǎ Chōng 贾充. He had held a multitude of titles in the service of the Cáo Wèi emperors during the Three Kingdoms period. And thanks to his loyal service and his association with Sīmǎ Yán 司马炎, the dynasty founder, Jiǎ Chōng was a high-ranking official.

01:51   You may recall Jiǎ Chōng's daughter Jiǎ Nánfēng 贾南风 from one of the sayings from last season, Gǒu Wěi Xù Diāo 狗尾续貂. She was the no good empress of the dim-witted and ill-fated Emperor Huì 晋惠帝.

02:06   The story behind today's saying comes from this time: Mù Rén Shí Xīn 木人石心. Let's quickly look at the four characters that make up this chéngyǔ.

02:16   Mù means wood.

60

CHINESE SAYINGS BOOK 3
EPISODE 9

02:18 | And a rén is a person or people. Or in this case, a man. Mùrén 木人, a wooden man.

02:26 | Shí 石 means a rock or stone.

02:29 | And Xīn means heart.

02:33 | So Mù Rén Shí Xīn. Wood Man Stone Heart. And those four characters were ascribed to our hero today. And his name was Xià Tǒng 夏统.

02:43 | Now, Jiǎ Chōng was a real person and has a Wikipedia entry and everything. But Xià Tǒng, he was a fictional person. Or maybe not. But he did make it to the Book of Jìn.

02:55 | He was originally from the Xiāoshān 萧山区 area of Hángzhōu but on this day when our story takes place, when he crossed paths with the official Jiǎ Chōng, he had his boat moored to the west bank of the Luò River that ran right through the center of the ancient capital of Luòyáng.

03:13 | On this day when fate brought these two men together, Jiǎ Chōng was out and about with his entourage enjoying some recreation and they decided to have a party right on the banks of the Luò River. And after they made themselves comfortable this official espied Xià Tǒng sitting in his boat pensively staring straight ahead. And Jiǎ Chōng saw that the boat seemed to be overflowing with all these medicinal herbs or plants.

CHINESE SAYINGS BOOK 3
EPISODE 9

03:44 | While everyone was engaged in a high state of merriment near a pontoon bridge that crossed the Luò River, Xià Tǒng remained on his boat, completely oblivious of them, continuing to stare straight ahead, paying them no mind whatsoever. Jiǎ Chōng was intrigued. There was something about Xià Tǒng that struck a nerve with him. And he wondered who is this person with such a grave expression, so unmoved by this whole scene going on all around him, not even looking up to notice them or acknowledge their presence.

04:19 | Jiǎ Chōng got out of his carriage and walked towards the riverbank, determined to find out more about him. He began engaging Xià Tǒng in some friendly conversation, asking his name, where he came, from and from this small talk and chit-chatting, Jiǎ Chōng could tell this young man Xià Tǒng seemed like no ordinary person.

04:44 | He asked Xià Tǒng what was he doing in town. Why had he come to the capital, over a thousand kilometers away to the northwest from his hometown in Zhèjiāng province? Xià Tǒng explained that his mother was deathly ill and he had come all this way to the capital to procure some medicine. This explained the dried herbs and what-not that filled up his boat.

05:08 | Jiǎ Chōng inquired why such a seemingly intelligent and capable guy like him lived out in the sticks and hadn't tried to make it in the city and perhaps become an official. Xià Tǒng grew somber and his mood changed at once. He said the life of an official serving in the government wasn't for him. He said he knew all about

CHINESE SAYINGS BOOK 3
EPISODE 9

the evils perpetrated by government officials for the sake of power. Politics wasn't his cup of tea. He had become fed up with the ways of people and society and yearned for a life that was pure and that embraced all the old values.

05:48 So he explained he had become a hermit and couldn't have been more content and satisfied living a quiet existence down in Xiāoshān. In fact, Xià Tǒng told Jiǎ Chōng, the sooner he left the capital the better. And he was just getting ready to start heading home.

06:05 Jiǎ Chōng decided to have a little fun. As their little encounter warmed up, Jiǎ Chōng requested a few things of Xià Tǒng. For example first he tested him how well he could steer his boat in the middle of the Luò River. Xià Tǒng thereupon proceeded to exhibit his precision handling of his vessel and everyone, not just Jiǎ Chōng, was impressed with his skills and the way he maneuvered his boat.

06:32 Then he asked Xià Tǒng to sing for everyone a song from his hometown. Xià Tǒng thereupon began singing a song that harkened back to the times of Yǔ the Great 大禹, the legendary Xià Dynasty founder and the fabled Cáo É 曹娥 who, as the legend goes, died in 143 trying to save her drowning father. All the swells lounging comfortably on the riverbanks were moved to tears by Xià Tǒng's singing.

07:03 Jiǎ Chōng hopped on board Xià Tǒng's boat and decided to test him further. In their short time together he

CHINESE SAYINGS BOOK 3
EPISODE 9

had become utterly enthralled by Xià Tǒng and was determined that this young man give up this nonsense down in his hometown and join him in the capital to serve the Jìn Dynasty emperor.

07:24 Back in those days, becoming an official in the imperial government was just about the highest hope one could have in life. Yet Jiǎ Chōng, one of the highest ranking officials in the land, personal friends with the Sīmǎ royal family, he couldn't convince this principled guy to say "I'm in."

07:45 He stood next to Xià Tǒng and thought of a way to get through to him. Knowing full well about the aspirations and weaknesses of men, Jiǎ Chōng thought he'd tempt Xià Tǒng with promises of power. At once he yelled out to his soldiers who guarded the whole noble entourage and shouted out orders to execute a number of drills and maneuvers. They did so in the most meticulous and precise fashion and Jiǎ Chōng turned to Xià Tǒng and said, "Look at that, my boy. Come join me in the government. Become an official and you too will have such power to command men. Xià Tǒng couldn't have been more unfazed by this display of power and didn't change his expression.

08:32 Okay, power didn't impress him. But Jiǎ Chōng came up with another idea. He called out to the bevy of singing girls who were partying with the group on the riverbank, to provide entertainment. And he ordered them to sing, dance and to amuse Xià Tǒng and perhaps arouse him with their beauty and sensualness.

CHINESE SAYINGS BOOK 3
EPISODE 9

08:54 | They danced right there at the waters edge, giving it their all. And Jiǎ Chōng nudged Xià Tǒng and said, "Look at that my friend. No ordinary man can behold such women. Come join me in the government and you can enjoy their beauty and charms anytime."

09:15 | Yet Xià Tǒng just stared ahead as bored as can be, completely unmoved by what he had just witnessed. Nor was he taken in by Jiǎ Chōng's words, clearly wishing for this to end so he could turn his boat around and start heading back home.

09:32 | Jiǎ Chōng threw up his hands in disgust and hopped out of Xià Tǒng's boat and roared, "This punk is made of wood and has a heart made of stone." He was a Mùrén, a wooden man who had a shí xīn, a stone heart. And everyone there who was on hand that afternoon to witness the events were moved and spoke of this encounter to others in the capital. And word spread about this principled man who remained so true to his morals and principles and what mattered to him in life. And that no amount of money, sensual pleasure or power could sway him.

10:12 | And Xià Tǒng became an inspiration to others as well who were pure of heart and refused to deviate from their chosen path in life, even in the face of the most powerful temptations that the material world had to offer.

10:28 | Jiǎ Chōng called him a Mù Rén, a wood man with a Shí Xīn, a heart made of stone. And people would pass around the story of the high-ranking Jìn Dynasty official,

Jiǎ Chōng, and the kid from Xiāoshān in Hángzhōu who couldn't be bought or seduced away from his chosen path in life.

10:51 If you are someone like Xià Tǒng, who commits themselves to a cause or profession, even if it doesn't bring you fame, wealth or material comforts and you never lose sight of your objectives even in the face of the most powerful temptations for an easier or more pleasure-filled life, you're the Xià Tǒng type. A mùrén shíxīn. You can't be bought. You're someone too principled to yield to temptation that might take your eyes off the prize you have committed yourself to achieve.

11:25 Later on in the Sòng Dynasty this mùrén shíxīn term was also applied to those who were utterly lacking in emotion or love or compassion. They are uncaring and had a heart made of stone. So at first this mùrén shíxīn term was used in a positive way. But later on it also came to be used to describe people considered cold-hearted and unfeeling.

11:53 Better to be the former than the latter, I say, if you're the mùrén shíxīn type at all. And with that, we will call it a day. As I said before, there's a whole lot more where that came from.

12:05 That's all I got. Laszlo Montgomery here, thanking you for listening, and signing off from Fantastic LA in the state of California, admitted into these United States back in September of 1850, first year in the unhappy

CHINESE SAYINGS BOOK 3
EPISODE 9

reign of the Xiánfēng 咸丰 Emperor.

12:25 I hope you enjoyed this little chengyu. If you did, then think about joining us next time for more words of wisdom at The Chinese Sayings Podcast.

Chinese Sayings Book 3
Episode 10

YOU ASKED FOR IT

开门揖盗—Kāi Mén Yī Dào

TRANSCRIPT

00:00 | Greetings everyone to the Chinese Sayings Podcast. This is Laszlo Montgomery bringing you another nice chéngyǔ for your ever expanding collection.

00:10 | For our ninth chengyu for this fifth season, I'm happy to present to you one that you can use over and over. This one's useful in situations where you want to tell someone If they do something they shouldn't, or perhaps don't do something they should, they're gonna regret it later on.

00:28 | And our selection this time is kāi mén yī dào 开门揖盗. Opening the door to invite a bandit inside, the Chinese equivalent of the English, to be asking for trouble.

00:40 | And boy, does this one ever have a fine provenance. It comes to us from the Book of Wú 三国志-吴国, one of the three books that make up the Records of the Three Kingdoms, the Sān Guó Zhì, written during the Jìn Dynasty 晋朝. And many years later in the 14th century, Luó Guànzhōng 罗贯中 wrote The Romance of the Three

CHINESE SAYINGS BOOK 3
EPISODE 10

	Kingdoms based on this ancient work of historiography.
01:04	Let's quickly look at the four characters and then get to the story behind it.
01:08	Kāi mén yī dào.
01:12	Kāi means to open and mén is a door. Kāi mén, open the door.
01:16	Yī, this is interesting. Now we don't do this in Western culture and I never experienced my first Yī until I started to become familiar with Chinese culture and mixed regularly with people from China or Greater China. When you Zuò Yī 作揖, you're bowing and also extending your hands before you and clasp them. It's one of these great human gestures that became custom in China. And because you would Yī 揖 to a person when you greeted them, in this instance Yī means to welcome someone or welcome them into your residence.
01:51	And a Dào 盗 is a robber or bandit.
01:55	Open the door welcome the bandit. Asking for trouble. And without further ado, let's look at the story taken from the Records of the Three Kingdoms from the Book of Wú.
02:06	There are five main characters to this story, straight out of the last years of the Eastern Hàn and Three Kingdoms era. And the two most important ones were the brothers Sūn Cè 孙策 and Sūn Quán 孙权. Now without delving

CHINESE SAYINGS BOOK 3
EPISODE 10

into the whole history of the Three Kingdoms, Sūn Quán was one of the three leaders contending for power to wear the mantle once worn by dynasty founders Yíng Zhèng 嬴政 and Liú Bāng 刘邦.

02:33 But Sūn Quán was not the one who was bound for glory and destined for greatness in his own time. The real hero in the family was his older brother Sūn Cè. The problem with Sūn Cè was that after establishing himself in and around Jiāngsū as a warrior and consequential military man, he died suddenly at the age of twenty five. This was in the year 200. The Eastern Han had twenty more years of life before Emperor Xiàn 汉献帝 capitulated to Cáo Pī 曹丕 in 220.

03:07 So this is what happened. I told you Sūn Cè got written out of the script very early in the events leading up to the Three Kingdoms period. During the 190's he really began to ramp up what later became the Kingdom of Wú. This is the Jiāngdōng 江东 region, those lands in China's east that have the Yángzǐ River running through them. Today, these are the richest and most productive lands in China.

03:34 Wú Prefecture 吴郡 had its capital city at Sūzhōu. That's where Sūn Cè chose to build his base. There, in this area known as Dōng Wú 东吴, Eastern Wú, he built his military base. He proceeded to gather stores of food and trained his armies in preparation to expand Eastern Wú lands.

03:58 The prefect of Wú, a man named Xǔ Gòng 许贡, became concerned about Sūn Cè's growing influence in

CHINESE SAYINGS BOOK 3
EPISODE 10

the region. So alarmed was Xǔ Gòng, he sent a secret message to the Han emperor, saying: 'Sūn Cè is a brave and fearsome man. I recommend that he be summoned back to the imperial capital, for his presence here in the provinces can only mean trouble.'

04:21 Unfortunately, however, Xǔ Gòng's messenger was intercepted by Sūn Cè's men. When the secret message reached Sūn Cè's eyes, he was furious. He immediately ordered that someone lure Xǔ Gòng to his manor. And when Xǔ Gòng stood before Sūn Cè he was seized, charged with conspiring against Sūn, and summarily executed by hanging. And other clients of Xǔ Gòng were also caught up in this whole thing and they too fared little better than their boss.

04:54 But Xǔ Gòng had three faithful followers who escaped the purge and were determined to avenge their former leader. They found out that Sūn Cè loved to hunt. One day, when Sūn Cè's hunting party set off for the mountains west of the town of Dāntú 丹徒, just south of Zhenjiang 镇江, these three avengers trailed him there.

05:17 Sūn Cè's horse was the swiftest and strongest of all the horses in the hunting party. Because of this, Sūn Cè quickly outpaced the rest of his hunting party by a great distance. As Sūn Cè, rode alone, chasing a deer, Xǔ Gòng's three followers set up an ambush and began their attack.

05:38 They caught up with Sūn Cè and one of them shot him through the cheek with an arrow. Caught by surprise, Sun

CHINESE SAYINGS BOOK 3
EPISODE 10

Ce's weapons clattered to the ground and he was only able to use his bow and arrow in self-defense, making a hasty retreat towards the rest of his hunting party.

05:57 Xǔ Gòng's three followers gave chase. But just as they were about to bear down on Sūn Cè, members of Sūn's hunting party rushed up to subdue and kill them. They carried their wounded leader back to his manor house to treat his ghastly wound.

06:14 But Sun Ce's cheek wound quickly became infected and his condition deteriorated. He knew that his days were numbered. He summoned his chief advisor Zhāng Zhāo 张昭 and others in his inner circle. He also called for his younger brother, still a teenager, Sūn Quán to his bedside to confer with them.

06:36 'We live in troubled times,' he said. 'But our area of Wú possesses excellent manpower and is securely situated on the banks of the Yangtze River. We should have nothing to fear. I ask you, my advisors, to give wise counsel to my younger brother when I am gone.'

06:56 He also handed a final letter to his brother Sūn Quán, which said, 'Out of us two brothers, I was the man more suited to raise armies, do battle, and conquer land. However, you are the man more suited to wisely utilize our manpower and resources in order to protect this land that has already been won.' Sun Quan, weeping profusely, accepted this final letter.

CHINESE SAYINGS BOOK 3
EPISODE 10

07:22 After Sun Ce's death, Sun Quan was devastated. This was a crushing blow to him. So sudden. He could think of nothing else and spent all his time weeping for the loss of his older brother.

07:36 Because of this, the advisor Zhang Zhao counseled him and said: 'Nowadays, the world is full of trouble and fighting and turmoil; greedy men vie with each other for pieces of land. If you continue to turn all your attention to grieving your brother, and let the affairs of your state go to seed, you are asking for trouble: it is just as if you are kāi mén yī dào. You're opening your door and politely inviting a bandit or a robber into your house.'

08:09 Zhāng Zhāo was telling Sūn Quán if he didn't stop his incessant weeping and mourning Sūn Cè's memory, he was inviting trouble into the front door. In these final years of the Eastern Hàn, his kingdom of Wú and the rich lands with so much abundance was going to be attacked by his enemies, of which he had a few. So using this saying, lifted from the Records of the Three Kingdoms, Zhāng Zhāo got Sūn Quán to see the light.

08:39 Upon hearing these wise words, Sun Quan rallied himself and began to tend to all the important matters related to his territory. And he took very effective measures to optimize everything begun by his elder brother Sūn Cè, including the continuous improvement of his military which would one day be engaged in a battle for the supremacy of China with the kingdoms of Wèi 魏国 and Shǔ 蜀国.

CHINESE SAYINGS BOOK 3
EPISODE 10

09:07 | Under Sūn Quán's leadership, beginning in 200, the state of Wú quickly became powerful, well-run and even more prosperous.

09:15 | So Sūn Quán was shell-shocked at first, all of eighteen years old when greatness got thrust upon him following Sūn Cè's death. Then after a dangerously long period of failing to rise to the occasion, shedding tears over his brother's sudden death, finally someone he trusted talked some sense into him. And comparing his inattention to matters of state to the act of inviting a robber into your house, he got through to young future Emperor of Eastern Wú.

09:46 | And that's the epic historical backdrop to Kāi Mén 开门, opening your door and Yī Dào 揖盗 inviting a bandit to come inside. The Chinese equivalent to the English 'Asking for Trouble', doing something they will later regret.

10:03 | Kāi Mén Yī Dào, a Chinese Saying coming to us from twenty one centuries ago and still being used today.

10:11 | Only a couple more to go in this fifth season. I extend to each and every one of you a big thanks for listening, and I hope you'll think about coming back next time for another satisfying episode of the Chinese Sayings Podcast.

Chinese Sayings Book 3
Episode 11

LIFE IS BUT A DREAM

黄粱美梦—Huáng Liáng Měi Mèng

TRANSCRIPT

00:00 | Hi Everyone, Laszlo Montgomery here with the Season Five closer. Wow, that was a quick twenty weeks.

00:09 | This Chinese Saying for today is pretty famous and comes to us all the way from the Zhěn Zhōng Jì 枕中记, The World Inside a Pillow. Other English names for this work include The Pillow Tale or The Dream on the Pillow. Popularly it's remembered as The Golden Millet Dream, among other names. And the genre of Chinese fiction that our chéngyǔ comes from is called Chuánqí 传奇.

00:36 | These Chuánqí stories originated from the Zhìguài Xiǎoshuō 志怪小说 stories that started showing up in the Hàn and evolved over the centuries leading up to the Tang Dynasty. This is a genre of Chinese literature filled with tales full of mystery and imagination, often containing all kinds of macabre and supernatural elements. The most famous person in the Chinese Pantheon of literary figures associated with these works

CHINESE SAYINGS BOOK 3
EPISODE 11

	was the early Qing Dynasty writer Pú Sōnglíng 蒲松龄.
01:10	This book, the Zhěn Zhōng Jì, is attributed to one Shěn Jìjì 沈既济 who lived 750-797. These were the years that included the Ān Shǐ Rebellion 安史之乱 as well as the reigns of Sùzōng 唐肃宗, Dàizōng 唐代宗, and Dézōng 德宗. Not the best years of the Tang Dynasty.
01:30	The Golden Millet Dream. Huáng Liáng Měi Mèng.
01:35	Huángliáng 黄粱 is a fine strain of millet. I don't think I've ever partaken of this stuff. Millet is a cereal crop that is embraced in developing countries mostly because it grows well in hot climates and has a short growing season. Not very demanding as far as agricultural crops go. India, China and Niger are the big three producers in the world.
02:00	Měi 美 is beautiful and mèng 梦 is dream. A měimèng 美梦, a beautiful dream.
02:07	Millet beautiful dream. This one has a nice long story attached to it, once again, taken from Shěn Jìjì's work the Zhěn Zhōng Jì, The World Inside a Pillow.
02:21	And it took place in the ancient city of Hándān 邯郸, once the capital of the State of Zhào 赵国 during the Zhōu Dynasty Warring States Period. It's one of China's most ancient cities going back to the Shāng, located in southernmost Héběi, not very far north of the Shāng Dynasty capital near Ānyáng. And this is all happening during the reign of Táng emperor Xuánzōng 唐玄宗, just

CHINESE SAYINGS BOOK 3
EPISODE 11

prior to the years author Shěn Jìjì lived.

02:52 There's more than one version of the story about the Golden Millet Dream. They're all basically the same narrative with different characters. It involves two men. One was a Daoist priest surnamed Lǚ 吕 and believed to be Lǚ Dòngbīn 吕洞宾, one of the Eight Immortals of Daoism. In another one of the stories Lǚ Dòngbīn is replaced by the other Immortal Zhōnglí Quán 钟离权. The other name I mostly came across for the priest was Lǚ Wēng 吕翁. Wēng 翁 means old man. So that'd be Old Man Lǚ. Whatever his name, he was a Daoist priest.

03:31 The other character was a scholar official named Lú Shēng 卢生. Like many people dissatisfied with their lot in life, Lú Shēng believed he had been given a bum rap. He was no longer a spring chicken, but he was still young enough to have a fire in his belly and felt heaven was working against him, denying him the life he aspired to.

03:54 Time had passed him by, and his work as a petty official in the civil service brought him neither wealth nor honor. In fact, Lú Shēng was barely getting by, living just enough for the city.

04:08 On the way back to his farm, Lú Shēng found himself in Hándān for the evening and looked for an inn to find shelter for the night. He had been on official duties and was on his way home to deal with matters back in his village.

04:23 So he pulled into this modest inn, paid his fee and was given a space on the floor and a mat of some kind to lay upon. Another fellow had already checked into the inn and Lú Shēng's space was adjacent to this man. This Daoist priest surnamed Lǚ.

04:44 So these two, they got on famously right from the start and they got to talking. In the course of their conversation, the priest asked Lú Shēng if he was doing well for himself. Lú Shēng at once grew bitter and proceeded to go on a rant about how tatty his clothes were and the meagerness of his traveling get-up. Then he bowed his head and sighed. He looked up and declared, 'By rights, I should be a successful and learned gentleman, but my ill fortune has reduced me to such undignified circumstances!'

05:15 Priest Lǚ replied, 'Why do you say your circumstances are poor? You are young with firm muscles and a healthy glow. Besides this, just now you were speaking in a lively manner and we were laughing happily. Why the sudden change in your tone?'

05:31 Lú Shēng said, 'Man, I'm only just getting by, not really living the good life like I should.'

05:38 'What do you mean by saying that your life isn't any good? 'asked Priest Lǚ. 'If you don't think your life is any good, then what sort of life would you like to lead?'

05:47 'I'll tell you,' Lú Shēng said, fixing his eye on the priest, 'Living well means winning fame for yourself and honour for your family.' He went on, 'It means being

CHINESE SAYINGS BOOK 3
EPISODE 11

a brave general in the army and a wise chancellor in the imperial court. It means that you host great feasts and hire dancing-girls to make merry with hundreds of honoured guests who all swarm to your abode at every opportunity. It means that your clan prospers and you are wealthy enough to satisfy every one of their needs. Only when one has achieved all this, can one be said to have led a good life.'

06:27　He went on, 'When I was young, I studied hard and learnt every skill necessary to achieve this sort of existence. I thought that, when I grew up, I would easily become a court official, decked out in splendid garments. But now that I am in the prime of life, I'm still worrying about insignificant things like the fields and the harvest. Was this my fate?'

06:52　Saying this, Lú Shēng sighed again, closed his eyes and proceeded to recline on the floor to take a nap. As this was all going on, the innkeeper was within eyesight and he was boiling up some millet for the evening meal. No one paid him any heed.

07:11　Priest Lǚ or Lǚ Wēng, he took a pillow out of his pocket and handed it to Lú Shēng, saying, 'Here, lay your head on this pillow. That will bring you good fortune, just like you wished for.'

07:24　The pillow was made of porcelain and had two small holes on either end. Lú Shēng rested his head upon it and fell into a slumber. In his dreams, the small pillow seemed to grow in size until the holes became big

CHINESE SAYINGS BOOK 3
EPISODE 11

enough and bright enough to walk through. Lú Shēng wriggled through one of the holes and suddenly found himself back home on the family farm.

07:50 Not long into this dream, after studying hard to become a scholar official, he was lucky enough to win the hand of one Miss Cuī 崔 from a neighboring town. Miss Cuī was not only beautiful, but came with a huge dowry. From that point on, Lú Shēng's circumstances began to improve rapidly. The next year, he passed the regional civil service exams with flying colours and was promoted to regional high office.

08:19 By now, he had cast off his old clothes of coarse cloth and put on official garments instead. The year after that, he entered the imperial civil service exams and was appointed the position of vice-prefect of Wèinán County 渭南 in east-central Shǎnxī 陝西. From there, he was promoted multiple times, until finally he worked directly under the Emperor, drafting speeches and imperial edicts. Then, he was given the important position of prefect of Shǎnzhōu District 陝州, western Henan Province.

08:53 As prefect, he worked avidly on improving his district's waterways. He oversaw the construction of more than eighty li 里 of canals in Shǎnzhōu, which made transport within the district much better. All the people under his jurisdiction loved and respected him. They even erected a memorial in his honour.

CHINESE SAYINGS BOOK 3
EPISODE 11

09:15 Later in his dream, he was transferred to posts in Biànzhōu 汴州, modern-day Kaifeng, and Lǐngnán (岭南) in the south of China, until he was finally promoted back to a post in the capital. At this time, the emperor was worrying over invasions from the Tibetan Tǔbō 土蕃 tribes on China's borders. The imperial army had just suffered huge losses in northwest Gānsù in Guāzhōu 瓜州 against the Tǔbō, and lost one of its best generals. The people of Guāzhōu were shaken and terrified.

09:47 To this newly vacant position of leadership in Guāzhōu, the Emperor saw fit to appoint Lú Shēng. In Guāzhōu, Lú led an army which broke through enemy lines and caused seven thousand enemy casualties. He re-occupied nine hundred li of territory and oversaw the construction of three major city walls. From then on, areas of military importance in Guāzhōu were well protected. The people of this area also admired and respected him, and recorded his great deeds by carving them in stone.

10:21 Lú Shēng returned to the imperial capital covered in glory. The emperor rewarded him handsomely and promoted him yet again. Because of his new promotion and his achievements, Lú was extremely popular with both the courtiers and the people.

10:38 But the emperor's prime minister started to become jealous of Lú Shēng and spread evil rumors about him. The emperor's mind was swayed and as it happened, Lú was demoted from his position in the capital to one in Duānzhōu 端州, southern Guangdong.

CHINESE SAYINGS BOOK 3
EPISODE 11

10:55 After three years, however, he was once again summoned to the capital and promoted until he performed some of the duties of the prime minister. He and two other officials held court for ten years as the emperor's most indispensable advisors. Because they were men of strong integrity who gave good advice, they were summoned to private audiences with the emperor multiple times a day. Lú was known for his wisdom and clear-sightedness and gained the moniker 'the Virtuous Minister', the xiánxiàng (贤相).

11:29 Once again, however, courtiers saw him enjoying all this favor and privilege and, as it was with every dynasty of every nation's history, there were those who became jealous or resentful of him. They spread rumors that he was conspiring with enemy tribes on the borders. And hearing such rumors, the emperor issued an edict that Lú was to be thrown into prison.

11:55 When messengers raced to Lu's abode with this news, he began to weep in panic. He said to his wife, 'I used to live on a few acres of good land in the area east of Xiáoshān 崤山, not far from Xī'ān 西安. I never had to worry about having enough to eat, or whether I would have a roof over my head. Why did I leave that simple life in order to pursue fame and fortune? Now I can only wish in vain for my old life, for my farming clothes of coarse cloth and my dark-colored little pony, on which I travelled the roads around Hándān!'

12:31 Saying this, he drew his sword to kill himself, but was prevented in the nick of time by his wife.

CHINESE SAYINGS BOOK 3
EPISODE 11

12:38 | Once in prison, all Lu's allies were killed. Lú himself narrowly avoided death only because some eunuchs put in a good word for him to the emperor. He was instead exiled to a distant, tropical southern province. But in a few years, the emperor learned that he had maligned Lú. He was once again summoned to the capital and given the title of the Duke of Zhào 赵国公. The emperor treated Lú very handsomely indeed to make up for his previous harshness.

13:11 | For example, Lú had five sons, and each of these five sons were given important positions in the imperial court. The youngest son in particular was both wise and virtuous, and was promoted to a high position at the age of only twenty-four. The Lú family made connections in marriage to families of great repute, and Lú had more than a dozen grandsons.

13:35 | Lú Shēng was then sent on two missions to Lǐngnán in the south from which he returned even more heavily lauded than before. He finally attained the position of prime minister. In his thirty-odd years at court, he gained honors and a reputation without rival in all the land. Now that he was old, he felt that he could enjoy his twilight years. The dancing girls in his abode were the most beautiful in China, and the emperor had given him countless rich fields, splendid palaces, and fast horses.

14:12 | But whenever he asked the emperor for permission to retire and return to his childhood home, it was denied. When Lú fell ill, he was waited on hand and foot by palace eunuchs, and the most famous doctors came to bring him the best medicines.

14:28 When he was close to death, he said, 'I was once a scholar in Hándān, and I spent my days ploughing the land and planting vegetables. One day, good fortune visited me. I became a court official, and was handsomely treated by the emperor. Although I am but a common man, I have given everything I have to serve him.

14:50 'Now, almost without realizing it, I have grown old. I am over eighty and have served many posts. I have come to the end of my life. I regret only that I have not been able to create some more glorious and lasting legacy for the emperor and the dynasty. With this regret, and with many thanks to the emperor for all his kindnesses, I must leave this world. Please pass my words on to the emperor.'

15:17 When the emperor heard this, he said, 'The Virtuous Minister became our prime minister based on his many talents and virtues. He calmed the borderlands and gave sage advice in court. That peace has reigned in China for twenty-four years is due in no small part to his efforts. Lately he has been plagued by illness, and just when we thought he was on the point of recovering, he sends word that his illness has grown more serious. We express our deepest sympathy and will send our best courtiers to visit him. We hope that he will take the medicines given to him, calm his thoughts, and focus all his energy on convalescing so that he can once again serve the court. We await the good news of his recovery.' That night, Lú Shēng passed away.

CHINESE SAYINGS BOOK 3
EPISODE 11

16:09 | Right at this moment, Lú Shēng stretched and woke up, raising his head from this porcelain pillow that the priest lent to him to find himself still on the sleeping-mat in the inn. Old Priest Lǚ was still sitting beside him, and the millet that the innkeeper was making for the evening meal was still simmering on the stove, not quite yet ready.

16:35 | Everything was just as he had left it. Like Dorothy waking up in Kansas on Aunt Em's farm, with Toto, Hunk and Zeke. And Lú Shēng asked the priest 'Was this all a dream?'

16:47 | Priest Lǚ replied with a smile, 'Life itself is like that dream!'

16:54 | Lú Shēng sat and pondered those words from this Daoist priest for a long time. Finally, he said to Priest Lǚ, 'I now know all the circumstances of that man's existence: his dreams and ambitions, his glories and despairs, his life and death. From this dream and what it teaches, I have now found a way to control my own discontent! I have learnt a great deal from you indeed!" Lú got up and ceremoniously kowtowed many times to Priest Lǚ. And without another word he got up and left the inn.

17:30 | And that's it. The end of the story. It's popularly known as the Golden Millet Dream because Lú Shēng dreamt his epic dream during the period of time it took the innkeeper to cook a pot of millet porridge. This story has been told and retold who knows how many times all over China and in the Chinese speaking world, going

CHINESE SAYINGS BOOK 3
EPISODE 11

back to the Táng Dynasty in the 8th and 9th centuries.

17:58　This Huángliáng Měi Mèng term became the Chinese equivalent of our English pipe dream. If you hear someone going on about something completely farfetched and unrealistic you can tell them that's just a Huángliáng Měimèng. A Golden Millet Dream. Your club is down seven nil and you're already into extra time but you think there still might be a chance? That's a pipe dream, a huángliáng měimèng.

18:25　So this is a popular Chinese Saying for anything that a reasonable person might find pretty impossible, but someone still believes it can happen. That's a huángliáng měimèng, a kind of hope or dream that is unrealistic, impractical, or unattainable.

18:44　And so we bring down the curtain on Season 5 here at the Chinese Sayings Podcast. I'll be back in four weeks with a whole new slate of chengyu's for you in Season 6.

18:55　Okay, I won't take up any more of your time. This is Laszlo Montgomery signing off from Los Angeles, as usual. And I thank you for listening and I look forward to seeing you again for another alluring episode of the Chinese Sayings Podcast

 Chinese Sayings Book 3
Episode 12

DO AS I SAY, NOT AS I DO

只许州官放火，不许百姓点灯—zhǐ xǔ zhōu guān fàng huǒ , bù xǔ bǎi xìng diǎn dēng

TRANSCRIPT

00:00 | Welcome back once again, peoples of this world, Laszlo Montgomery here with yet another good and decent chengyu for your collezione.

00:10 | This one is useful to know in our day and age where everyone carrying a cell phone can act like an intrepid journalist, catching criminals, celebrities and politicians in the act of engaging in all kinds of illegal or hypocritical acts.

00:26 | Now I don't regularly feature twelve character Chinese Sayings. In fact, I can't recall when I ever featured one. Let's break it down and see if we can figure it out.

00:37 | It goes like this: Zhǐ xǔ zhōu guān fàng huǒ, bù xǔ bǎi xìng diǎn dēng. As chengyu's go, that's quite a mouthful. So let me introduce it two characters at at time, since I know you're all busy and don't need to sit through a character by character analysis.

00:55   Zhǐ xǔ 只许 means only allowed or only permitted. A zhōuguān 州官, well a zhōu in China's olden days was what you called a prefecture and a guān is an official. So, a high ranking official who worked for the local government. Fànghuǒ 放火 means to set fire to something or commit arson. Zhǐxǔ zhōuguān fànghuǒ. Only allow government official to commit arson.

01:26   And now for the second part of the Chinese saying. Bùxǔ bǎixìng diǎndēng 不许百姓点灯. Bùxǔ 不许 means to not allow or not permitted. And bǎixìng 百姓? Bǎi means one hundred and xìng means a surname. The Bǎixìng or hundred surnames is a term used to express all the Chinese people who were not government officials.

01:44   Since, back in the time of this story at least, you could pretty much almost divide up the entire Chinese population into one hundred different surnames. That hundred surnames term just became another way of saying "the Chinese people", the masses, the Bǎixìng 百姓, the hundred surnames. Or Lǎobǎixìng 老百姓, the old hundred surnames.

02:08   And to diǎndēng 点灯 means to light a lantern or a lamp.

02:13   And when you string all six of those characters together you get Bùxǔ bǎixìng diǎndēng. Only allow government official to commit arson. Not permit the people to light a lantern.

02:24   Hmmm, I'm getting a real strong Boris Johnson, Nancy Pelosi, Bill de Blasio, and Gavin Newsom vibe right now.

CHINESE SAYINGS BOOK 3
EPISODE 12

02:32   The story behind this one doesn't go back that far. I'm usually mining the Zhōu, Hàn and Jìn dynasties for all these golden nuggets. But our chengyu for this time only goes back as far as the Northern Song, 960 to 1127.

02:50   And during that time of great poets, painters and calligraphers there lived one Lù Yóu 陆游. He had the ill fortune to have been born in 1125, the final years of the Sòng dynasty when the capital was at Kāifēng. By this time the Jürchens from in and around Manchuria were leaning hard on the imperial court and making all kinds of horrible demands. And after they milked the royal treasury for all it contained, they went in and smashed the dynasty to smithereens and carted off the whole royal family to the coldest most miserable part of Heilongjiang that they knew of. And there they all lived out the rest of their days. The famous Jìngkāng Incident 靖康事变 from Chinese history.

03:33   So Lù Yóu grew up in these troubled times. Despite all that, he went on to become perhaps the most prolific literatus of the dynasty, writing more than 11,000 poems. And like his contemporary whose life overlapped that of Lù Yóu, Yuè Fēi 岳飞, he was considered one of the great patriots of his time. And throughout his life, he called for the Sòng to rally its armies and retake the north of the country lost to the Jürchens who had established their own Jīn Dynasty 金朝. And like Yuè Fēi, Lù Yóu also ran afoul of Emperor Gāozōng's 宋高宗 evil chancellor, Qín Huì 秦桧.

CHINESE SAYINGS BOOK 3
EPISODE 12

04:13   Well, after living a long and eventful life, Lù Yóu retired to a quiet house by a lake, which he named the Abode of the Aging Scholar. There, he wrote a book called, coincidentally enough, Notes from the Abode of an Aging Scholar 老学庵笔记, Lǎo xué ān bǐ jì. In it, he included various notes on local traditions and ancient books he had read, as well as plenty of personal observations, memories, and strange stories he had heard from family or friends. This is one such story.

04:46   There once was a man named Tián Dēng 田登. He was a tyrannical and egotistical man who had managed to get himself appointed a prefect. One of the first things he did upon taking up his post was to put a ban on the use of the character Dēng 登, which was his first name. In ancient China, it was tradition to put a taboo on using the characters in the reigning Emperor's first name, out of respect for his majesty.

05:14   But this person, Tián Dēng, he was merely a regional official, a prefect, and certainly had no right to call for this taboo against using the character dēng. This was highly unusual and people thought, who is this guy? Being so presumptuous as that.

05:34   Nonetheless, everyone who lived under Tián Dēng's jurisdiction was not allowed to speak or write this character dēng 登. And not only that, Tián Dēng then put a taboo on any written character that had the same pronunciation as the word dēng. Not even the emperor, the Son of Heaven himself, not even he dared to do such a thing as that.

CHINESE SAYINGS BOOK 3
EPISODE 12

05:56 | If you check the Pleco App or the Liáng Shíqiū 梁实秋 dictionary, you'll see there's about five characters that are all pronounced dēng in the first tone. And a couple of them were pretty common and part of everyday speech.

06:12 | Nevertheless, whoever dared to say Dēng out loud would be charged with 'Disrespecting the Prefect'. If Tián Dēng was feeling forgiving that day, the one got caught uttering the forbidden syllable using the character dēng in the first tone, might be caned or beaten. And if Tián Dēng was in a lousy mood, the accused might even be sentenced to prison or executed. Many county officials met this fate due to unfortunate slips of the tongue.

06:43 | Not long after Tián Dēng took office, the annual Lantern Festival rolled around. The general word for any light or lamp in Chinese is Dēng 灯, which of course fell under Tián Dēng's taboo.

06:57 | And as you can imagine, it became nearly impossible to plan the upcoming Lantern Festival without being able to mention the word dēng. According to the traditions of that prefecture, it was left up to the prefect to host the annual Lantern Festival gala which lasted for three days.

07:15 | The staff at the prefect's residence wanted to put out notices advertising the celebrations, as they had done every year before. But this year, with the taboo on using any character with the pronunciation of Dēng, it was severely straining their ability to get the word out to the masses. If they wrote the word for 'lanterns', also pronounced dēng, they'd be punished for breaking the

CHINESE SAYINGS BOOK 3
EPISODE 12

taboo; if they didn't write 'lanterns', there was concern that it would confuse the people and they wouldn't comprehend the meaning of the notification. People were guaranteed to feel confused.

07:49 What to do? Eventually, after careful consideration, the officials decided to replace the character for 'lantern' dēng 灯 with the character for 'fire' huǒ 火. Therefore when they hung these announcements all over town, it didn't say 'The prefect will be putting on a lantern show for the town lasting three days', as was the wording used in years past. Instead this time the advertisements announced: 'The prefect will be setting fire or fànghuǒ 放火 to the town for three days'.

08:22 As soon as the notices were plastered in conspicuous locations where the people were sure to see it, there was immediate confusion regarding what this meant. Based on Tián Dēng's well-known personality and tendency to give ridiculous orders, no one put it past him to actually set fire to the town. The result was that there was a mass exodus from the town as the people hurried to flee what they thought would be a three-day-long fire.

08:50 And believe you me, a lot of the townsfolk grumbled that they weren't even allowed to have lights or lanterns for this year's festival because of Tián Dēng's taboo on the word Dēng. They argued about why was it that they couldn't light lanterns for this year's festival but no one stops the prefect from setting fire to a whole town!

CHINESE SAYINGS BOOK 3
EPISODE 12

09:08 News spread fast throughout the entire prefecture and surrounding counties about the lunacy being called for by the government officials. And from this we got the saying of, "the prefect commits arson, while the townsfolk cannot even light lanterns!"

09:25 And in no time at all this became an oft-used saying that satirized those in power who committed all sorts of wanton activities, while the common folk weren't even able to go about their daily lives. It literally translates to: The prefect commits arson, while the townsfolk cannot even light lanterns. It's the perfect chengyu to lampoon any person in power who disregards certain rules that they themselves call for or should be enforcing while the ordinary people live under the harsh restrictions.

09:57 With the recent Covid madness all over the world, in more places than the UK and the US plenty of government officials were making life unpleasant for the citizens with all the draconian restrictions about social gatherings. But they'd be caught red-handed breaking the rules. Lockdowns for thee but not for me.

10:17 When your boss demands you show up on time but they're always late, zhǐ xǔ zhōu guān fànghuǒ, bùxǔ bǎixìng diǎndēng.

10:26 Your spouse rags on you for not following certain rules in the relationship that they flaunt all the time? Zhǐ xǔ zhōu guān fànghuǒ, bùxǔ bǎixìng diǎndēng.

10:37	Anytime somebody hops up on a soapbox and starts yammering on about rules, laws, conduct and then they get caught on video being a hypocrite, zhǐ xǔ zhōu guān fànghuǒ, bùxǔ bǎixìng diǎndēng.
10:51	Yeah, we're not too fond of this kind of thing. And folks back in the 12th century, they weren't either. Do as I say, not as I do.
11:00	And with that we're going to close the window, bring down the curtain and turn out the lights until next time when we meet again, on the avenue.
11:09	This here's Laszlo Montgomery signing off from hot and sunny Los Angeles California, beseeching you to consider coming back next time for another useful chengyu, here at the Chinese Sayings Podcast.

 Chinese Sayings Book 3
Episode 13

SWEATING BUCKETS

汗流浃背—Hàn Liú Jiā Bèi

TRANSCRIPT

00:00 | Welcome back my friends to another Chinese Sayings Podcast. Laszlo Montgomery here with another good and decent chengyu. Another useful one if I may add with a most excellent provenance. Same as last time, Der große Historiker, Sīmǎ Qiān, the one who gave us the Records of the Grand Historian. The Shǐjì 史记, one of the best sources for fabulous Chinese Idioms.

00:26 | Today's Chinese Saying, Hàn Liú Jiā Bèi 汗流浃背, we can all relate to this one. And now that the summer is here and times are tense all over the world, this one's so useful, it belongs in your random access memory rather than putting it on a five and a quarter inch floppy disk.

00:43 | Hàn Liú Jiā Bèi. Let's break it down into its constituent parts. Hàn 汗 means sweat or perspiration. And Liú 流 means anything that flows, like water. So Hàn Liú 汗流 would mean the sweat was flowing. And Jiā 浃 means to wet or to soak or drench. And your bèi 背 is your back or the back of the body. Sweat flowing drench back. This

97

CHINESE SAYINGS BOOK 3
EPISODE 13

is one of those sayings you can sorta get it. You know where this one is going. It's meaning is clear.

01:16 So here's the story that Sīmǎ Qiān wrote about in a chapter taken from the Records of the Grand Historian called Chén Chéngxiàng Shìjiā-Prime Minister Chén Píng 陈丞相世家-陈平.

01:28 This is a good one because it revolves around the infamous Lǚ Clan Disturbance of 180 BC, a perennial favorite among lovers of popular Chinese history, with a little bit of the old ultra-violence. Empress Lǚ, I will go out on a limb here and declare she has got to make almost anyone's list of the top five most reviled royal figures in Chinese history. Empress Lǚ. Lǚ Hòu 吕后.

01:54 You see, she was the empress of the Hàn Dynasty founder, Liú Bāng 刘邦. We remember him also as Hàn Gāozǔ 汉高祖. When the Qin 秦 Dynasty up and died like it did, so suddenly in 210 BC, there were two main contenders for the control of the empire that Qín Shǐhuáng left behind. These were of course Xiàng Yǔ 项羽 of Chǔ 楚 and Liú Bāng of Hàn 汉.

02:19 Chén Píng was a capable fellow who had first served Xiàng Yǔ but defected to Liú Bāng and ended becoming one of his most trusted and indispensable advisors. In fact, Liú Bāng was so beholden to Chén Píng, he made him his chancellor when he began building his Hàn Dynasty.

CHINESE SAYINGS BOOK 3
EPISODE 13

02:38　When Emperor Gāozǔ died in 195 BC, Empress Lǚ was able to jump right in and install her eldest son onto the throne, the weak and feeble Emperor Huì of Hàn 汉惠帝. And she won't be the last empress dowager to do this, but with essentially no one but her in charge, she grabbed hold of the reins of power and ran the show in China for a good fifteen years until she died in 180 BC. Her son, Emperor Huì, according to Sīmǎ Qiān, was so terrified of his mother he dared not ever push back on anything she said.

03:17　And with no one to ever tell her no, Empress Lǚ was able to control most of the affairs of state. She could even call a deer a horse if she wanted to. And she proceeded to stuff the imperial court with all her Lǚ family relatives as princes and ministers of China. If there was a plum position, it went to one of her kin.

03:39　And when poor old Emperor Huì finally breathed his last at the tender age of twenty-four in 188 BC, Empress Lǚ declared herself regent for a new child emperor that she had installed on the throne. And for eight more years she ruled the Han Empire. And when she finally reached the end of her days, one of her final acts was to name two of her Lǚ clan relatives field marshal and prime minister of China. She also gave these two relatives control over the Han empire's southern and northern armies respectively. She played the long game and had made it her mission to maintain absolute power over the empire her husband had founded by controlling all the most powerful and important offices.

**CHINESE SAYINGS BOOK 3
EPISODE 13**

04:26 | And Empress Lǚ accomplished this by having all these important positions within the Han empire filled by members of the Lǚ clan, and not the founders of the Han Dynasty themselves, the Líu 刘 clan.

04:40 | The court ministers loyal to the Hàn Dynasty watched this state of affairs with great anxiety. But while Empress Lǚ still lived, they dared not make any moves against her. But now that she was gone, one minister named Zhōu Bó 周勃 finally decided it was time for action. With the support of Chén Píng 陈平, Hàn Gāozǔ's loyal advisor, Zhōu Bó led a sustained military campaign that wiped out each and every one of the Lǚ's from power.

05:12 | Then once the Lǚ's were neutralized, Zhōu Bó and Chén Píng wisely installed Emperor Gāozǔ's son by another wife. This son was named Líu Héng 刘恒. Líu Héng would go on to become the renowned Emperor Wén of Hàn 汉文帝. One of China's truly great emperors.

05:31 | Emperor Wén would be followed by his son, Emperor Jǐng, another great Hàn emperor. And rounding out this trifecta of great emperors was Emperor Jǐng's son who reigned fifty-four years as the consequential Emperor Wǔ 汉武帝. And together, this father and son and grandson were called by many, among China's greatest emperors.

05:55 | When Emperor Wén first ascended to the throne, he rewarded Zhōu Bó and Chen Ping by naming them co-prime ministers, rewarding them for their role in squelching the Lǚ Clan.

CHINESE SAYINGS BOOK 3
EPISODE 13

06:07 | Now, with that long historical introduction out of the way, here's the story behind our chengyu for this time.

06:15 | Chén Píng took to affairs of state like a fish to water. He was a natural at delegating, keeping accounts, and presiding over judicial matters. Zhōu Bó, on the other hand, he was a military man through and through and not so handy behind a desk. But now that there was peace throughout the land, Zhōu Bó's martial skills were no longer needed. But in his new role as co-prime minister he found himself way out of his element, not to mention his comfort zone.

06:46 | One day early in his reign, Emperor Wén held court in order to familiarize himself with his country. He addressed Zhōu Bó first: "Minister, can you inform me how many criminal cases were tried in the Hàn courts this year?"

07:00 | Zhōu Bó had no idea and could only shake his head in reply. Then Emperor Wén asked again, "Minister Zhou, can you tell me how much the Hàn court collected in grain and silver, and how much were the public expenditures?"

07:14 | Once again, Zhōu Bó hadn't a clue. Now, here's where we get this Chinese Saying.

07:21 | Poor old Zhōu Bó began to sweat profusely from all the pressure. Emperor Wén was asking him all these detailed questions and he couldn't answer even a single one. And everyone was watching him. The shame and embarrassment he felt caused his body to sweat. And it flowed down his back and drenched his imperial court robes as Emperor Wén asked him question after question. And all of them he could not answer.

07:48　Finally, Chén Píng stepped in to rescue his colleague. "Your Majesty, I've delegated matters of criminal justice to a minister of justice; and matters of income and expenditure to a minister in charge of the treasury. Why don't you summon them, since these are their areas of expertise, and they'll be able to answer your questions at once."

08:08　Emperor Wén was extremely pleased with Chén Píng's answer, and no longer questioned Zhōu Bó. Zhōu Bó breathed a temporary sigh of relief. But that day, when he got home from the palace, he submitted a request for early retirement. His inability to answer even one of Emperor Wén's questions clearly showed that he was not suited for this kind of work. Instead, he had already served the Hàn Dynasty to the best of his abilities, by leading the military action against the Lǚ clan and restoring the Liú family to power.

08:44　So after the appropriate honors were paid to Zhōu Bó, and he had been properly thanked for his service to the empire, he made a graceful exit stage-right, not unlike Cincinnatus back in 458 BC. Chén Píng ended up taking over as the only prime minister and served the emperor well. As for Zhōu Bó, history remembers him favorably for his key role in restoring the fortunes of the ruling Liú clan and in restoring them to power. So you can say

CHINESE SAYINGS BOOK 3
EPISODE 13

Chén Píng really served Liú Bāng not only before he became emperor but long after he was gone as well.

09:21 We have terms like sweating buckets, sweating like a pig, pouring with sweat. When you're walking down some street on a late August day or night, you too might be Hàn Liú Jiā Bèi. Any time you are schvitzing in a terrible way. Hàn Liú Jiā Bèi.

09:38 Yes, this common chengyu gets taken out of its wrapper and used for any occasion that calls for it. And next time you use it, remember the sweaty appearance of poor Zhōu Bó who was forced to endure a grilling from no less a personage than Hàn Emperor Wén.

09:55 So this is where we get the Chinese saying Hàn Liú Jiā Bèi 汗流浃背. You use it to describe either yourself or someone else soaked with sweat from the sweltering temperature or from being in the hot seat in a given situation.

10:09 And that my good friends, is going to be that. This is Laszlo Montgomery, signing off from hot and sweaty Los Angeles, California. Hàn Liú Jiā Bèi. Trust me when I say I'll be back again, once more with feeling, for another useful episode of the Chinese Sayings Podcast.

Chinese Sayings Book 3
Episode 14

THE COMEBACK KID

东山再起—Dōng Shān Zài Qǐ

TRANSCRIPT

00:00 | Welcome back, ladies and gentlemen! Laszlo Montgomery here with another nice flavorful and nutritious Chinese Sayings for you. We're halfway through the season. Times flies when you're having fun. Or as one might say it in Chinese, Guāng Yīn Sì Jiàn 光阴似箭. Time flies like an arrow.

00:19 | But that is not our Chéngyǔ for this time. Today we have another swell one that comes to us straight from the Book of Jìn 晋书, compiled during the Táng Dynasty. As you know, it was always the succeeding dynasty that would compile the official history of the preceding one, giving credence to the old saying that the past is what happened and history is how it's written about.

00:43 | Our Chinese saying for this episode is Dōng Shān Zài Qǐ 东山再起. And as we always seem to do, and for good reason I suppose, let's break these four syllables down.

CHINESE SAYINGS BOOK 3
EPISODE 14

00:53 | Dōng 东 means east and shān 山 means mountain. Eastern Mountain.

00:58 | Zài 再 means again or once more.

01:02 | And qǐ 起 means to rise, get up or stand up, among other definitions.

01:08 | Dōng Shān Zài Qǐ. Eastern Mountain again rises.

01:14 | Well, I guess that can mean anything so let's hop in our time machine and go back more than sixteen centuries ago to the time of the Eastern Jìn Dynasty when the capital was located down in Jiànkāng 建康, modern-day Nánjīng. This is where the Jìn royal family ended up after getting brutally chased out of their previous capitals of Luòyáng and Cháng'ān by the marauding tribes from the north.

01:40 | During the Eastern Jìn Dynasty, there lived a scholar named Xiè Ān 谢安 who lived 320-385. He was also known as Xiè Dōngshān. Dōngshān again, meaning Eastern Mountain.

01:53 | Even at a young age Xiè Ān was famous for not only his intelligence and high degree of learning, but also as a rather proficient calligrapher. As a young man, he was offered a position in the bureaucracy reporting directly to the prime minister. This was a position in the capital that offered many opportunities for advancement in the government.

CHINESE SAYINGS BOOK 3
EPISODE 14

02:15 But, like many other intellectuals of the time, Xiè Ān had no desire for government work. This was a common theme throughout Chinese history: the talented literatus/scholar who, though eminently qualified, rejected a life in the government bureaucracy so that they may engage in the lifestyle of a traditional Chinese scholar.

02:38 Despite his feelings about not wishing to work in the government, Xiè Ān finally got talked into serving as an official in the Eastern Jìn government. But not long after, he feigned sickness, quit his job, and moved back to his hometown in Kuàijī 会稽. Now, this city of Kuàijī, later on in 1131 during the early Southern Sòng Dynasty was renamed Shàoxīng, a city very much renowned for its scholars and literati. And its wine.

03:10 But Xiè Ān had become too famous and renowned to lead the secluded life he wished for. Upon hearing once that Xiè Ān was in the vicinity, the Prefect of Yángzhōu 扬州 himself came to offer him a nice position in that city. Xiè Ān initially refused, but the prefect was rather persistent and so, after plenty of arm twisting, Xiè Ān had no choice but to accept the offer.

03:36 But not more than a month or so later, Xiè Ān manufactured another excuse to resign and left this government job as well. And in the years to follow, Xiè Ān kept dodging attempts from the government to serve as an official.

03:52 Rather than involve himself in the bureaucracy, Xiè Ān lived a nice leisurely life, writing poetry with his friends and fellow intellectuals such as Sūn Chuò 孙绰 and Wáng Xīzhī 王羲之. These two were among the most renowned and celebrated poets, calligraphers and literati of their day. Wáng Xīzhī was covered in an old China History Podcast episode number 96. He is immortalized in Chinese cultural history as perhaps China's greatest calligrapher and for his legendary "Introduction to Poems composed at the Orchid Pavilion." a.k.a. The Lántíngjí Xù 兰亭集序.

04:34 Though Xiè Ān and his friends often toured the south, taking in China's magnificent scenery and landscapes, his home base remained a mountain called Dōngshān in Kuàijī, again, present day Shàoxīng, northeastern Zhèjiāng province.

04:51 One day, as he sat on the mountain looking out over the rivers and valleys below, Xiè Ān sighed contently: 'How lucky I am to be able to lead the life of the ancient hermit, Bóyí 伯夷!' Bóyí was a mythical figure from the most ancient times.

05:09 Meanwhile, Xiè Ān's younger brother Xiè Wàn 谢万 was rising quickly in the imperial court, doing what his older brother refused to do, serving in the government. As talented as Xiè Wàn was, everyone acknowledged that it was really brother Xiè Ān who was the real genius of the two. The further up Xiè Wàn managed to climb, the more everyone lamented that Xiè Ān had gone into seclusion.

05:38 Seeing that Xiè Wàn's family was growing rich after his

CHINESE SAYINGS BOOK 3
EPISODE 14

many promotions, Xiè Ān's wife grew discontented with her own husband's simple lifestyle. She went to Xiè Ān and complained: 'Can you call yourself a great man if you keep hiding away from fame and fortune?'

05:56 But Mrs. Xiè had no better luck than the government officials who kept trying in vain to entice Xiè Ān to leave his perfect life of solitude and scholarship behind and to go work for the Eastern Jin imperial court.

06:10 Not long after that, Xiè Wàn, as it often was at the pinnacles of power, came up short in a political struggle and, as punishment, was stripped of all his titles and demoted to commoner status. This shook Xiè Ān greatly as it reflected badly on the Xiè family name. So he was determined to do something to restore the family's honor. Therefore, already forty years old, Xiè Ān reluctantly agreed to accept a position as a military commander under the great general Huán Wēn 桓温.

06:44 The day Xiè Ān left his home in East Mountain to take up his position, many important officials came to give him a big sendoff. One official joked, 'How many times the imperial court has tried to entice you back! We never thought we'd see the day you'd come off your high horse on East Mountain.' Xiè Ān smiled and bowed modestly at his friends praise. And off he went to serve at his post, which he did with the expedited competency.

07:10 A little later on, General Huán Wēn started getting imperial aspirations and was counting on Xiè Ān's loyal support in the political struggle that was sure to happen.

CHP CHINESE SAYINGS BOOK 3
EPISODE 14

07:24 | But Xiè sided with the general's rival claimant to the throne and for this, he earned Huán Wēn's enmity.

07:32 | A potential showdown occurred in 373 when General Huán Wēn marched on the capital, ostensibly to seize power from the Eastern Jìn emperor. At such a politically dangerous time as this, those in the capital Jiànkāng were shaking in their boots about Huán Wēn and his army seizing power.

07:52 | But Xiè Ān remained as cool as a cucumber and welcomed his political rival who he had sided against in the power struggle, risking his life in the process. He convinced Huán Wēn to give up these thoughts of seizing power. And as it happened, this all became a moot point after Huán Wēn died later that year in 373. Nothing came of this political trembler. Xiè Ān later on took measures to break up General Huán's power base and the political crisis was resolved. From there, Xiè later went on to become the prime minister for the Eastern Jìn emperor.

08:31 | As prime minister Xiè Ān governed wisely and was lauded for his wisdom and fairness. But this time in Chinese history, late fourth century, it was anything but a peaceful and stable time from the fall of the Western Jìn and into the period of the Sixteen Kingdoms.

08:47 | If you look at the China map of the 380's AD, you'd see the Eastern Jìn only controlled the southern half of China and the Former Qín occupied the northern half. In line with most of these northern kingdoms, the rulers of Former Qín were not Hàn Chinese. This state was ruled by people of the Dī tribe 氐族 of northern nomadic tribesman, one of the so-called Wǔhú or Five Barbarians who got all the credit for bringing down the Western Jìn and for causing one of the first waves of mass migration to the south of China of these Northern Han Chinese, many of which later became known as the Hakka people.

09:28 Well, come 383 AD the Former Qín emperor, he was determined to make a go at conquering Eastern Jìn and unifying China in the process. And when the battle drums started being beaten, the people in Eastern Jin were wringing their hands and terrified at what was to come. Xié Ān, as prime minister, acted as a calm oasis in a storm, directing matters and, though technically not a military man, he prepared for the defense of the capital. And this gave the people confidence. Even the military officers were having a bit of a freak out but again, seeing Xiè Ān seemingly in control and almost indifferent at the dangers gave his men hope.

10:13 And all lovers of Chinese military history know that everything led up to the Battle of Féi River 淝水之战, November 383. Former Qín made its move and it's believed somewhere perhaps in Ānhuī west of the capital Héféi, the famous Battle of Féi River went down. And the upshot was a victory for Eastern Jìn. And so utterly complete was the Eastern Jìn victory, the Former Qín never recovered and didn't last much longer, falling in 394. The Eastern Jìn on the other hand, they lived on until the year 420 whereupon they got replaced by the Liú Sòng Dynasty, first of the Southern Dynasties.

CHINESE SAYINGS BOOK 3
EPISODE 14

10:56 So it's from this story that we get Dōng shān zài qǐ. Xiè Ān, who lived on Dōngshān, East Mountain, present day Shàoxīng. He had reluctantly served in the government but retired to a life of seclusion and even took on the name Dōngshān, Xiè Dōngshān. But after he retired from his service, he was called upon to serve China at a dangerous hour in history, and for that comeback after he had already retired, he is remembered in this Chinese saying taken from the book of Jin that told how Dōngshān, Xiè Ān's other name, zàiqǐ, rose again.

11:35 And for anyone who resigns or retires from the stage and makes a comeback, we can use this chéngyǔ of Dōngshān Zàiqǐ. No matter politician, general, movie celebrity, like Robert Downey Jr. for example. A big star and part of the Brat Pack in the 1980s. He faded from the scene after all his personal issues, but Dōngshān Zài Qǐ, he made a comeback and enjoyed a nice run in the Iron Man franchise of movies. Tony Bennett too, Dōngshān Zàiqǐ. What a comeback he made in the 1990s!

12:11 America's 6th president John Quincy Adams, after serving in the hot seat from 1825 to 1829, came back half a dozen years later to serve brilliantly as a member of the US House of Representatives. Dōngshān Zài Qǐ.

12:26 How about Dick Nixon? After the 1962 presidential election he declared you wouldn't have Nixon to kick around anymore. But Dōngshān Zài Qǐ, he made a great comeback and later went on to become the 36th president.

CHINESE SAYINGS BOOK 3
EPISODE 14

12:42 | After the failed Gallipoli Campaign of 1915, Winston Churchill's career was finished at the age of forty. But Dōngshān Zài Qǐ, he rose again in 1940 and went on to become one of the great men of history.

12:56 | You don't have to be famous or a historical figure. Any one of us, when it's seemingly all over for you, but later you rise again and make a comeback in your career or in your personal life, Dōngshān Zài Qǐ.

13:10 | Okay, this one ran a little long but don't hold it against me, I beg you. From the city of LA in the El Dorado State, this is Laszlo Montgomery signing off, wishing you a fond farewell and asking you once again to come back next time for another alluring episode of the Chinese Sayings Podcast.

Chinese Sayings Book 3 Episode 15

A BLESSING IN DISGUISE

塞翁失马—Sài Wēng Shī Mǎ

TRANSCRIPT

00:00	Good afternoon ladies and gentlemans, Laszlo Montgomery here back again with the seventh installment of the 6th season of the Chinese Sayings Podcast. Glad you can make it.
00:12	Another good one today. Another quickie, with both a four and eight character version. Like the golden oldie from the very first season of this Chinese Sayings Podcast, Qiānlǐ Sòng É'máo 千里送鹅毛, there's a short version and a long version. If you utter the first part only, that'll do the trick.
00:33	The short version for today's chéngyǔ is Sài wēng shī mǎ 塞翁失马. And if you wanted to add the second part, you follow Sài wēng shī mǎ up with four more characters: yān zhī fēi fú? 焉知非福.
00:44	And with that all said, let's put this one under the microscope.

CHINESE SAYINGS BOOK 3
EPISODE 15

00:50 Sài wēng shī mǎ.

00:52 Sài 塞 is a place of strategic importance, a fortification or the frontiers of the Chinese empire that was always prone to attacks from nomadic tribesmen.

01:03 Wēng 翁 is an old man but used in a courteous or respectful manner. Some of you may recall Lǚ Wēng 吕翁 from the Season 5 closer Huáng Liáng Měi Mèng, Old Man Lǚ.

01:14 Shī 失 means to lose.

01:17 And a mǎ 马 once again is a horse, not a deer.

01:21 Sài wēng shī mǎ. Frontier old man lose horse. Who knows what that means? Let's see if the back four characters shine any light on this. Yān zhī fēi fú 焉知非福.

01:32 Yān 焉 is a pronoun used in classical Chinese meaning here or this. And in rhetorical questions it means how. Zhī 知 means to know.

01:43 Fēi 非 means wrong or a wrongdoing.

01:48 Fú 福 is one of the most important Chinese characters. A lot of people wear jewelry with this character on it or hang in in their house of upside on the outside of their door. It means good fortune or blessings. It's also a tattoo favorite.

So the Frontier old man lose horse. In what respect know

CHINESE SAYINGS BOOK 3
EPISODE 15

is not a blessing?

02:09　Let's not hit the buzzer yet. I already kinda tipped you off but before we blurt out the answer, let's harken back to the good old days of the Western Hàn Dynasty and open up the ancient classic book the Huáinánzǐ 淮南子 to the chapter entitled Rénjiān Xùn 人间训. The Duke of Huáinán: Lessons from The People. The Huáinánzǐ was a work containing a bunch of scholarly debates carried out at the residence of the Prince of Huáinán that sought to argue the best possible ways to order society and what makes the perfect ruler. The Huáinánzǐ is heavily influenced by Taoist philosophy, and also contains Confucian overtones.

02:51　So let's dive right in and listen to the story behind this one. It's a short one.

02:57　Living in a frontier town of the Chinese empire was an old man who was skilled in divination and fortune-telling. One day, this elderly gentleman's horse wandered outside the borders of China, into the territory of the nomadic tribesmen who often mounted attacks on Chinese towns. This was no small thing for horses were like your car, your tractor and were a critical part of your household and well-being. Wandering into enemy territory like it did meant the old guy couldn't dare go look for it.

03:28　Everyone gave the horse up for lost, and some came to offer their sympathies to the old man to comfort him for his loss. But the old man said to his well-wishers, "How

CHINESE SAYINGS BOOK 3
EPISODE 15

do you know that this matter might not turn out to be a stroke of good fortune?" That gave everyone pause to wonder and some no doubt appreciated the old man's positive mental attitude.

03:52 After some months, to everyone's surprise, the old man's horse returned. And not only did his horse return but accompanying it was another very fine horse who had most likely once belonged to some tribesman of the steppe.

04:05 Now, seeing the old man's good fortune, everyone came to offer him their heartiest congratulations. Yet the old man said to his visitors, "How do you know that this whole thing might not end badly? Why are you so sure this is a stroke of good luck?" The people considered what he said and thought, perhaps.

04:23 Now that the old man had two good horses, not only he but his only son as well, they could both go out riding together. But one day on one of these trips, something spooked the horse ridden by his son and it rose up in fear, throwing the son his mount. The son broke his leg from the terrible fall. And such was the injury he suffered, never again could he walk normally and his leg never fully recovered.

04:52 All the local townsfolk heard about this and came to offer their sympathies and tried to comfort the old man on this misfortune that befell his son. As they uttered their kind words and sought to make him feel better, they found him utterly unconcerned, and if fact, calm

CHINESE SAYINGS BOOK 3
EPISODE 15

and smiling as if this was all nothing. He went on to say "How do you know this broken leg might not be a blessing in disguise?" Once again the people silently wondered about these words he had spoken.

05:22 A year later, the nomadic tribes from the north launched a full-scale invasion of the Chinese border towns. As was the common thing to do back then, every able-bodied young man was called upon to take up arms and defend Chinese territory. But such was the ferocity of the nomad invasion that of every ten Chinese men who went out to meet them in battle, nine did not return.

05:47 Of course, the old man's only son, with his bad leg, had not been able to go fight in the war. And for this reason, when the old man became feeble and infirm in last years he still had his son to take care of him for the rest of his days.

06:02 From the story behind this Chinese Saying of this old man, Sài wēng shī mǎ, we can see what might seem like good or ill fortune might turn out to be just the opposite. And what seems unlucky might in fact be fortuitous. In the Huáinánzǐ it's written: Huà bù kě jí shēn bù kě cè yě 化不可及深不可测也 The changes of life are innumerable and their depths are beyond human prediction.

06:33 So this chéngyǔ gets trotted out anytime you hear someone so accepting of their ill or good fortune. You never know if something that appears to be a setback or a disaster, later on turns out to be one of the best things that ever happened to you.

CHINESE SAYINGS BOOK 3
EPISODE 15

06:48 Sài wēng shī mǎ, yān zhī fēi fú. An old man loses his horse, how do you know this isn't a blessing? But all you have to say if the front four: Sài wēng shī mǎ. That's what you use whenever you want to say that something might be or indeed was a blessing in disguise.

07:07 Sài wēng shī mǎ, yān zhī fēi fú. Or if that's too much of a mouthful, Sài wēng shī mǎ will suffice in expressing your belief that something might be or ended up being a blessing in disguise.

07:23 And there you have it. Our seventh Chinese Saying of the season. Three more to go before we take our usual post CSP season Caribbean vacation.

07:36 This is Laszlo Montgomery signing off from LA California, as always, wishing you a fine farewell and tempting you to come back next time for another useful and interesting chéngyǔ, here at the Chinese Sayings Podcast.

Chinese Sayings Book 3
Episode 16

I WAS MADE TO LOVE HER

家徒四壁—Jiā Tú Sì Bì

TRANSCRIPT

00:00 | Good evening everyone, all you chéngyǔ lovers around this watered world of ours. Laszlo Montgomery here, as always, with a nice meaningful Chinese Saying to add to your ever-expanding collection. Fifty-eight of them, already and still tens of thousands to go yet.

00:18 | And in this episode we're looking at Jiā Tú Sì Bì 家徒四壁, a nice one lifted from the Hànshū 汉书, the Book of Hàn. Boy, does the Hàn Shū deliver or what? Quite a hefty repository of chéngyǔ's from the Book of Hàn. Five already including this one that made it to the CSP so far.

00:39 | In this Chinese Saying I'm going to introduce a figure from ancient times who is making his first appearance on this show, namely, Sīmǎ Xiāngrú 司马相如. Don't confuse him with the Warring States legend from Zhào, Lìn Xiāngrú 蔺相如, who we featured in three past episodes Wán Bì Guī Zhào 完璧归赵, Fù Jīng Qǐng Zuì 负荆请罪 and Jiàzhí Liánchéng 价值连城. So much did Sīmǎ Xiāngrú admire this great politician and general

CHINESE SAYINGS BOOK 3
EPISODE 16

	from Zhào, he took on his personal name, Xiāngrú 相如.
01:13	But before we go any further, let's quickly break down the four characters and see if we can guess what this one's all about.
1:20	Jiā Tú Sì Bì 家徒四壁.
01:23	Jiā 家 is a home or your family.
01:26	And the character, Tú 徒, when used as an adverb means empty or bare.
01:32	Sì 四 is the number four and a bì 壁 is a wall.
01:37	Home empty four walls. I think we can guess what this Chinese Sayings is used for. But then again, looks can be deceiving. So let's hear the story that comes to us from more than twenty-one centuries ago from the Book of Han chapter entitled the Biography of Sīmǎ Xiāngrú. 汉书·司马相如传.
01:58	Sīmǎ Xiāngrú lived during the 2nd Century BC. He was a learned man from the city of Chéngdū 成都 in Shǔ Prefecture 蜀郡 in the heart of Sìchuān province. He's revered as one of Chengdu's famous sons. By all accounts Sīmǎ Xiāngrú was considered a child prodigy, as he was clever, studious, and a talented swordsman to boot. He was the whole package.
02:25	And as the years passed, his genius only increased. He excelled at the most popular forms of Chinese literature

CHINESE SAYINGS BOOK 3
EPISODE 16

in his day, namely a kind of poetry called cí and fù, cífù 辞赋. The Cí form of poetry, in the style of the great poets of 3rd and 4th century BC Chǔ State were wildly popular during the Han Dynasty. The Fù poems or rhapsodies were also greatly appreciated in their day. And Sīmǎ Xiāngrú, he is still generally considered the greatest writer of cí and fù literature of all time.

03:06   But Sīmǎ Xiāngrú, unlike a lot of great literati, came from a background of abject poverty. His one stroke of luck was that he was discovered by Wáng Jí 王吉, the county magistrate of Línqióng 临邛, a neighboring county to the southwest of Chengdu. I spent a few days there once, myself.

03:23   Wáng Jí became friends with Sīmǎ Xiāngrú and generously provided him with living quarters, and treated him as an honoured guest of the county government. Wáng Jí also went to visit Sīmǎ Xiāngrú every day and to further help him, talked Sīmǎ Xiāngrú up in front of other powerful men, always praising Sīmǎ Xiāngrú's talent in front of them.

03:45   There were two great tycoons of the Línqióng area who were named Zhuó Wángsūn 卓王孙 and Chéng Zhèng 程郑. When they heard that the county magistrate, Wáng Jí had a protege such as Sīmǎ Xiāngrú, a jewel of a man, they fell all over themselves to invite Sīmǎ Xiāngrú to their own banquets and events so that they could impress all their connections and business contacts.

04:09   But Sīmǎ Xiāngrú repeatedly declined their invitations time and again. He accepted only when his friend, Magistrate Wáng, implored him to make an appearance at Zhuó Wángsūn's upcoming banquet.

04:24 At a soiree one night hosted by Zhuó Wángsūn, Sīmǎ Xiāngrú's flair for poetry, his wit, and his sparkling conversation dazzled all of the host's important guests. Zhuó Wángsūn was extremely satisfied. All the trouble he had gone to, to get Sīmǎ Xiāngrú to show up, had been worth it. As the evening went on, Magistrate Wang asked Sīmǎ Xiāngrú to perform for them on the qín, and Sīmǎ Xiāngrú obliged. Of course, he played masterfully and all the guests applauded and called for an encore.

05:02 But before Sīmǎ Xiāngrú could begin, he heard the tinkling of jade bracelets from the direction of the women's quarters. And a beautiful girl's face could be seen peeking out from behind the screen that divided the women from the banquet guests. This girl was none other than Zhuó Wénjūn 卓文君, the daughter of the host Zhuó Wángsūn. She had been married off very young but her husband had passed away. So, following Confucian tradition, she had returned to her father's house to remain a chaste widow for the rest of her life, bringing her dowry back with her.

05:38 Zhuó Wénjūn herself, was an accomplished and well-read woman, and moreover a true music lover. Sīmǎ Xiāngrú's playing had so entranced her that she had forgotten her place and strayed out of the women's quarters.

CHINESE SAYINGS BOOK 3
EPISODE 16

05:52 | What else can I tell you except that it was love at first sight for Sīmǎ Xiāngrú and Zhuó Wénjūn. A flash of inspiration came to Sīmǎ Xiāngrú, and his fingers, which had been poised to begin another song, began strumming the chords of The Phoenix Seeks His Mate Fèng Qiú Huáng 凤求凰. This was a song about a man confessing his love to a woman, and upon hearing this, Zhuó Wénjūn understood Sīmǎ Xiāngrú's meaning immediately.

06:22 | In the spirit of true love, she knew she had to follow him wherever he went. Against her father's strong opposition, and against all the societal taboos against a widow remarrying, Zhuó Wénjūn eloped with Sīmǎ Xiāngrú, back to his hometown of Chengdu.

06:40 | Zhuó Wénjūn had been a rich man's daughter her whole life and never wanted for anything. When she entered the threshold of her new home, she had never seen anything like the conditions in which Sīmǎ Xiāngrú lived. His home contained barely more than four walls. Jiā Tú Sì Bì 家徒四壁.

06:59 | Nevertheless, she had resolved to become Sīmǎ Xiāngrú's wife, for richer or poorer, and in sickness and in health. And never once, in all the time they spent together, did she ever utter a word of complaint about living this rough. Instead, she and Sīmǎ Xiāngrú came up with a plan. Now this whole matter of Zhuó Wénjūn eloping with Sīmǎ Xiāngrú was a huge loss of face for her father. In his anger, he cut all ties with his daughter and refused to let her see a penny of her dowry.

CHINESE SAYINGS BOOK 3
EPISODE 16

07:33 | Not daunted at all, Zhuó Wénjūn and Sīmǎ Xiāngrú moved back to Línqíong. Of course, this time they were no longer the honored guests of Magistrate Wáng. His reputation took a hit, being the one who introduced Sīmǎ Xiāngrú and all.

07:50 | What these two lovers and soulmates did to sustain themselves was to open up a tavern right in the middle of town. Zhuó Wénjūn herself was busy all day serving all manner of rough-and-tumble tavern guests, instead of remaining behind a screen as befitted a rich man's daughter. And Sīmǎ Xiāngrú manned the counter and did the accounts. At night, together, side by side, they cleaned and washed up the dirty dishes right in the middle of the street, where everyone could see. And they felt not a lick of shame and cared not what anyone thought of the humble circumstances of their life. Anyone consumed with love and devotion to their one true love, nothing else matters.

08:37 | If Zhuó Wángsūn thought having his widowed daughter remarry was shameful, he very nearly died of shame when she became an alewife on a busy thoroughfare in the middle of the town where he lived. Just to get rid of this blot on his reputation, he agreed to give his daughter her dowry on the condition that she never return to Línqíong.

08:59 | Zhuó Wénjūn was more than happy with this arrangement, and she and Sīmǎ Xiāngrú returned to Chengdu where they purchased a large plot of land and lived very comfortably from that point forward.

CHINESE SAYINGS BOOK 3
EPISODE 16

09:10 Later on, no less a person than the great Hàn Emperor Wǔ noticed Sīmǎ Xiāngrú and invited him to his royal court where he became an exalted figure there. In the end Zhuó Wénjūn was filled with joy that her gamble of defying her father paid off so well.

09:28 The love story of Zhuó Wénjūn and Sīmǎ Xiāngrú, with its elements of forbidden romance, defying outdated traditions, and outwitting a local fat cat, has become an extremely popular folktale, recurring again and again in operas, novels, and folksongs.

09:48 And in the Chinese tradition, to describe someone who is extremely poor, one could say jiā tú sì bì, his house contained only four walls. And people who would hear these words would recall the great love story of Zhuó Wénjūn and Sīmǎ Xiāngrú. But would also know they didn't have much and could only afford to live in humble circumstances.

10:13 Jiā tú sì bì. A home containing only four walls. A chéngyǔ that describes a state of extreme poverty like Sīmǎ Xiāngrú's humble abode.

10:24 And, like with many a chengyu, you can also use this one when someone compliments your home. You can exhibit a nice dose of false modesty by retorting, oh, Jiā tú sì bì, playing down their compliment.

10:39 So we end on a high note. It's always nice to hear stories like this one. So much more pleasant than Chinese sayings that came from stories of deceit, war or murder.

CHINESE SAYINGS BOOK 3
EPISODE 16

I'll take a happy ending whenever I can get them

10:52 Jiā tú sì bì. An empty home with nothing except four walls. You can use this one to describe yourself or anyone who's living rough and barely making ends meet. Jiā tú sì bì. I hope no one can say this about themselves.

11:08 And that is gonna be it for this time. On behalf of the crew here, this is Laszlo Montgomery signing off from Los Angeles, California, in the middle of a drought. I thank you for listening and may I cordially invite each and every one of you to come back again next season for another refreshing and healthy chéngyǔ, here at the Chinese Sayings Podcast.

Chinese Sayings Book 3
Episode 17

WE SWORE BLOOD BROTHERS AGAINST THE WIND

桃园结义—Táo Yuán Jié Yì

TRANSCRIPT

00:00	Welcome back everybody, Laszlo Montgomery here with you for a third time this season, bringing you another golden oldie and well-known favorite of many a lover of Luó Guànzhōng's 罗贯中 14th century novel, Romance of the Three Kingdoms. Anyone who read that book is surely familiar with this story behind today's Chinese Saying. Táo Yuán Jíe Yì 桃园结义.
00:25	Before I get into the story, let me mansplain these four characters.
00:29	Táo Yuán Jié Yì.
00:31	A Táoyuán 桃园 is a peach garden. Táo 桃 is peach and a yuán 园 is a garden.
00:36	A Jié 结 is a knot or to tie or weave something. It also means to settle or conclude some matter.
00:44	And Yì 义 means about a dozen things. Relationship,

CHINESE SAYINGS BOOK 3
EPISODE 17

friendship, justice, among them. But a Jiéyì 结义 means to become sworn brothers.

00:53 I suppose it can just as well means sworn sisters but our story that goes along with these four characters Táo Yuán Jié Yì, concerns three men.

01:04 So without further ado, let's get to this great story that serves as yet another magnificent shining star in the galaxy of Chinese culture. Without dredging up the whole sorry ending of the Han Dynasty, suffice to say, by the early 3rd century AD, incompetence and a collection of unsavory characters in the imperial government, combined with a terrible famine and peasant unrest, stirred up massive discontent among the common folk. Those are often the essential ingredients for fomenting rebellion.

01:39 Three brothers from Jùlù 巨鹿 raised a peasant force that grew into five hundred thousand rebels from all over Eastern China. This sizable army, was recognizable by the yellow head cloths or turbans they wore. And they had proclaimed: 'The mandate of Heaven has passed from the Han; the time of the Yellow Turbans is at hand.' Cāng tiān yǐ sǐ, huáng tiān dāng lì 苍天已死, 黄天当立.

02:02 And in popular Chinese history, this Yellow Turban Rebellion ended up being the proverbial final straw, the final nail in the coffin that led to the extinction of the Eastern Han.

02:17 In a prefecture called Yōuzhōu 幽州, today's Liaoning

CHINESE SAYINGS BOOK 3
EPISODE 17

Province and a bit of northern Hebei, there came news that the Yellow Turbans were approaching. The prefect of Yōuzhōu hastily summoned the marshal of his army. The marshal told the prefect: "Our forces are few, and the Yellow Turbans are many. The speediest way of raising an army is to put out notices summoning men to our cause."

02:43 Following this advice, the prefect immediately had recruitment notices posted far and wide throughout Yōuzhōu. One such notice was posted in Zhuó County 涿县, today's area around Bǎodìng 保定, Hebei Province. A heroic looking man stood before the notice and sighed deeply. He was a man of few words; fond of reading, calm and generous in temperament, and stoic of countenance.

03:10 He was a great-hearted man, who especially loved to meet and befriend other heroes of the land. Believe it or not, he was seven feet tall, with earlobes that touched his shoulders and arms that reached past his knees. His face was like white jade and his lips like red rouge. He belonged to a fallen branch of the Han imperial family. His lineage of the Liú family had sunk into poverty in Zhuó County some time ago. His name was Liú Bèi 刘备.

03:43 Losing his father as a child, Liú Bèi had been brought up in a very simple way by his mother, and now scraped out a living by weaving straw mats and sandals. As a boy, Liú Bèi had lived in a house underneath a magnificent mulberry tree, whose splendid canopy could be seen for many miles round. The people nearby would whisper to each other, "The household under the mulberry tree is sure to produce nobility."

04:12 One day as the child, Liú Bèi was playing with the other children of the neighborhood, his uncle happened to pass by and heard Liú Bèi say, "When I am Emperor, I will ride a carriage with a canopy just like that mulberry tree." From then on, his uncle knew that Liú Bèi would grow up to be no ordinary man, and for this reason, though he was of small means, he supported Liú Bèi and his mother whenever he could.

04:41 When Liú Bèi was fifteen, his mother sent him to travel throughout China and study, and he became friends with many wise and accomplished men on his journey.

04:51 In the year the prefect of Yōuzhōu put out notices seeking men for his army, Liú Bèi was twenty-eight years old. And when he had read the notice fully, he gave a great sigh. Suddenly he heard a loud voice from behind, sternly saying: "And why does a hero like you heave sighs instead of going to serve his country?"

05:13 Liú Bèi turned around to look at this person who had just accosted him. This man, no kidding, was eight feet tall, with two-foot long sideburns. He had a head like a leopard, whiskers like a tiger, a voice like thunder, and a posture like a racehorse. Liú Bèi saw at a glance that he was extraordinary, and immediately asked for his name.

05:38 "My name is Zhāng Fēi 张飞," said the man, "and generations of my family have lived in Zhuó County. We

CHINESE SAYINGS BOOK 3
EPISODE 17

own plenty of land here, and I myself make a living as a wine and meat-seller. But what I like best is to meet and befriend heroes of the land. That is why I spoke to you when I saw you sighing over the notice."

05:58 "I am of the same Liú family as the Han royalty, and my name is Liú Bèi. Today I heard of the Yellow Turban Rebellion. And although my greatest wish is to help restore peace to the land, I am not fully equipped to do it. That is why I stand and sigh."

06:15 Zhāng Fēi replied, "Well, if that is all, I have plenty of resources, and in fact I myself am trying to raise an army from our county. What do you say you and I do this together?"

06:25 Liú Bèi agreed most wholeheartedly and the two men went into a tavern to talk over their plans.

06:31 As they huddled together over their bowls of wine, they saw a burly man rest his wheelbarrow against the front of the tavern. Then this man entered through the doorway and yelled, "Waiter, bring me some food and wine, for I am going this minute to the city to volunteer for the army."

06:48 Liú Bèi took a closer look at this man. He was even bigger than Zhāng Fēi, standing nine feet tall, and he had two-foot long sideburns. His face was the color of a date, and his lips red as rouge. He had eyes like a phoenix, and was altogether a man of striking and imposing appearance. Liú Bèi at once invited him to his

	table and asked his name.
07:12	The man replied, "My name is Guān Yǔ, and I am originally from Hédōng 河东. But I killed a powerful man there who used his position to exploit the poor. And thus I had to escape, and I have been a jiānghú 江湖, wandering the land for five or six years. Today I happened to be here when I heard of the Yellow Turbans, so I am heading out to join the army."
07:34	Liú Bèi told Guān Yǔ of his and Zhāng Fēi's mutual intentions, and Guān Yǔ was most delighted to hear this. They talked long into the night, and when the tavern closed, they removed themselves to Zhāng Fēi's house to discuss matters further.
07:50	Zhāng Fēi said, 'In the back of my house is a peach orchard, where the blossoms are just now blooming. What do you two say that tomorrow, we meet in the peach garden to make sacrifices to heaven and earth, and declare ourselves blood brothers? We all have the same ambition, and this oath we take will bring us closer together in our plans."
08:10	Liú Bèi and Guān Yǔ approved the plan in one voice. And the next day, the three men met in the peach garden, with a black bull and a white horse as sacrificial animals. Lighting sticks of incense, the men made this vow: "We are Liú Bèi, Guān Yǔ, and Zhāng Fēi. Though we do not share a surname, we vow to be brothers for life, and to work towards the common goal of helping the destitute.

CHINESE SAYINGS BOOK 3
EPISODE 17

08:36 We will bring honour to the Heavens above and our families on Earth. We did not ask Heaven to be born on the same day; but we ask you now to grant our wish that we should all die on the same day. If any of us renounces this vow, may he be struck down by Heaven!"

08:55 So they met in a táoyuán, a peach garden and declared a jiéyì, a sworn brotherhood. And upon the conclusion of this Táoyuán Jiéyì ceremony, they became a sworn brotherhood of three heroes of the future Shǔ Hàn Kingdom 蜀汉国, immortalized for eternity in the great classic novel, Romance of the Three Kingdoms.

09:19 After they had sworn this vow, the three men recognized each other as brothers: Liú Bèi as the eldest, Guān Yǔ as the middle brother, and Zhāng Fēi as the youngest. And when the sacrifices had been made, they slaughtered another head of cattle and gathered three hundred men in the peach garden to drink and feast. The next day, they and their men gathered up their equipment and went to join the army to fight the Yellow Turban rebels.

09:46 So this most famous part of the Romance of the Three Kingdoms can be used in instances that describe any band of people, doesn't have to be three, and you don't have to be joining together to go fight a massive peasant rebellion either. Any group of people who have common objectives and interests and who solemnly join together to fulfill a common goal, no matter to achieve an objective or to declare everlasting loyalty, can add an adult dose of gravitas and solemnity to their vow by harkening back to this great moment in Chinese literature.

CHINESE SAYINGS BOOK 3	
EPISODE 17	

10:22 | The Records of The Three Kingdoms, the Sānguó Zhì 三国志, doesn't specifically mention this Peach Garden incident but it does say that the three men, Liú Bèi, Zhāng Fēi and Guān Yǔ were as close as brothers. So this may or may not belong in the realm of Chinese historiography. But as far Chinese culture, this story sits in the front row.

10:44 | And that is gonna be that for this time. I thank you for listening. This is Laszlo Montgomery signing off from Los Angeles, California, as usual, inviting you to come back next time for another satisfying episode of the Chinese Sayings Podcast.

Chinese Sayings Book 3
Episode 18

I CARRY THE BURDEN AND SHAME

忍辱負重—Rěn Rǔ Fù Zhòng

TRANSCRIPT

00:00 | Welcome back my friends to the Chinese Sayings Podcast. Laszlo Montgomery with you once again, bringing you another jewel of a chéngyǔ. One I may say that mixes well with our previous selection from this season, Táo Yuán Jié Yì.

00:16 | The story behind our chengyu for this one too, takes place during those fabled decades lasting from 220-280, when the once unified China was broken up into the three kingdoms of Shǔ Hàn 蜀汉, Cáo Wèi 曹魏, and Eastern Wú 东吴. Plenty of gilded chengyu's came out of that age. Including this one: Rěn Rǔ Fù Zhòng 忍辱负重. This is one of those idioms that, when we break it down, sorta gives the meaning away. But such a great story! How could I not tell it.

00:47 | Rěn Rǔ Fù Zhòng. Let's give it a once over.

00:51 | Rěn 忍, as a verb means to bear or endure or put up with.

CHINESE SAYINGS BOOK 3
EPISODE 18

00:56 And rǔ 辱 means disgrace, dishonor as a noun or a verb.

01:01 Fù 负 means to carry on the back or shoulder or to shoulder or bear.

01:08 And Zhòng 重 means weight or weighty in the sense of important.

01:12 Endure disgrace carry a heavy burden on your back or a weighty responsibility. Well, you can get the main idea but without attaching a story to it, these are just mere words. So, let's all grab our copies of the Sān Guó Zhì 三国志 off the shelf once more with feeling, the Record of the Three Kingdoms to the Wú Shū 吴书, the Book of Wú, to the chapter on The Life of Lù Xùn 三国志·吴书·陆逊转. Not the great 20th century literary figure, Lǔ Xùn 鲁迅. Our hero for this story was surnamed Lù 陆 not Lǔ 鲁. And he was a major figure in the Kingdom of Eastern Wú.

01:50 So, the story goes like this. Following the decisive Battle of Red Cliffs, 208-209 AD, conditions were ripe amongst the Three Kingdoms for direct confrontation. Following this Battle of Red Cliffs, Cáo Cāo's 曹操 mighty Wèi army was taken down a few pegs and less of a threat. But tensions between Sūn Quán 孙权 of Wú and Líu Bèi 刘备 of Shǔ were only intensifying.

02:17 Sūn Quán wanted back a territory he had temporarily leased to Shǔ. This was Jīngzhōu 荆州, located in southern Hubei. But Guān Yǔ, who had been assigned by Líu Bèi to guard the territory, refused to return the land.

CHINESE SAYINGS BOOK 3
EPISODE 18

02:32 | So, while Guān Yǔ 关羽 was away doing battle with Cáo Cāo's forces in Xiāngyáng 襄阳, today's Hubei's second largest city, Sūn Quán took his officer Lù Xùn's 陆逊 advice and mounted a sneak attack to regain Jīngzhōu.

02:47 | When Guān Yǔ hurried back to defend the territory, he was killed by Sūn Quán's forces. When this news reached Líu Bèi, he was furious, and right then and there vowed to avenge Guān Yǔ's death by destroying the state of Wú. Ignoring the advice of his best officials, including Zhūgě Liàng 诸葛亮, he led more than a hundred thousand troops in a full-scale eastwards invasion of Wú.

03:13 | This new state of affairs caused Sūn Quán much anxiety. He recognized that this was a matter of life or death for Wú: its borders were threatened from the north by Cáo Cāo, and now, encroached upon by Líu Bèi from the west as well.

03:29 | In an effort to halt the oncoming invasion, Sūn Quán sent multiple emissaries to try and reason with Líu Bèi. After all, Sūn Quán and Líu Bèi had allied together to defeat Cáo Cāo at the Battle of Red Cliffs. But each time, Líu Bèi, still mourning the death of his sworn bother Guān Yǔ, rebuffed Sūn Quán's overtures, and the Shǔ army continued its advance further into Wú lands.

03:58 | At this crucial juncture, Sūn Quán realized that there was only one general who could save Wú. This was his go-to guy for all important and critical matters, Lù Xùn. He assigned a force of fifty thousand men to accompany Lù Xùn, with orders to meet Líu Bèi's forces head to

CHINESE SAYINGS BOOK 3
EPISODE 18

head in battle.

04:19 Before Lù Xùn set off, Sūn Quán took off the precious sword hanging at his own side and presented it to him, saying, "Use this well in your camp."

04:31 At the time, Lù Xùn was still quite a young man. Besides, he came from a scholarly background. Joining him to lead the Wú forces were experienced generals, many of them well-connected among the aristocracy, who had seen battle since the days of Sūn Quán's elder brother, Sūn Cè 孙策. Of course, to these generals, Lù Xùn was a mere upstart and they grumbled about why did he get this important command.

04:57 By 222 AD, Liú Bèi's force of well over a hundred thousand men had penetrated five or six hundred li 里 into Wú territory. Liú Bèi's army had also managed to besiege one of Sūn Quán's best generals, his own nephew Sūn Huán 孙桓, in Yídào 夷道, also in today's Hubei Province.

05:17 Meanwhile, when this news reached Lù Xùn, all the other generals with him advised him to go to Sūn Huán's aid. Lù Xùn, however, said confidently: "General Sūn is perfectly capable of directing his troops during a siege, and the fort of Yídào is well-supplied. We need to focus on winning here. If we do that, Sūn Huán's problem will solve itself." The generals did not argue with Lù Xùn's decision, but they were uneasy at heart.

CHINESE SAYINGS BOOK 3
EPISODE 18

05:46 | Lù Xùn pitched camp at Yílíng 夷陵, also in Hubei, a critical position right across from the camp of the Shǔ forces. He ordered his men to begin building fortifications and defenses right away.

06:00 | The Shǔ forces, seeing Lù's army camped right across from them, began itching for a battle. Every day, they came up close to the Wú camp, yelling all manner of insults and trying to goad the Wú forces into violence. But Lù Xùn refused to send so much as a single Wú soldier to engage the Shǔ army. Eventually, his generals grew impatient and flooded into Lù Xùn's tent, all but ordering him to give the command to engage.

06:30 | Lù Xùn would not budge. He said, "Líu Bèi's forces are flush with victory from their advance east into Wú borders. Their morale is high and they occupy an advantageous position. We will never succeed in routing them if we attack now. All we can do is strengthen our own position and wait for the right moment." At this, the generals broke out into a storm of protesting. They thought Lù Xùn was behaving in a cowardly manner and being too overly-cautious for first refusing to help break Sūn Huán out of his siege, and then for refusing to engage the belligerent Shǔ Hàn army. So loudly did the generals argue that Lù Xùn had to slap the table for attention. "I may be a scholar and not military men like you," he said, "but I was chosen by the commander-in-chief for one reason: and that is, I can endure any indignity, and bear any responsibility, to see this mission out to a successful end.

CHINESE SAYINGS BOOK 3
EPISODE 18

07:33 | That's right. This is where Lù Xùn let it be know he was willing to Rěn Rǔ Fù Zhòng 忍辱负重. He was just fine with suffering these insults from Shǔ for the sake of the ultimate objective, that being, defeating them in battle.

07:48 | Lù Xùn continued, "My orders are not to engage, and anyone who goes against my will can contend with the commander-in-chief's sword." Saying this, he unsheathed the sword Sūn Quán had given him. Although the generals were still unhappy, no one wanted to go against such a threat.

08:09 | And so, for four long months from February to June, the Wú army did not emerge from their encampment, and did not respond to the Shǔ army's taunts. In June, the famous Hubei weather began to change and it grew unbearably hot. In order to escape from the relentless Hubei sun, Líu Bèi had to lead his forces away from the open into a forested area to seek shade. By this time, the Shǔ forces were spread out amongst forty interconnected camps stretching across seven hundred lǐ of Wú territory. That about 375 kilometers.

08:48 | This was the moment that Lù Xùn had been waiting for. The weather was hot and dry, and the Shǔ forces were spread out way too thinly over too large a space. Lù Xùn waited for a night when the wind was in the east, and began his attack.

09:05 | He had an advance guard of men sneak up on the Shǔ camp with bundles of kindling, and at a single command, all the bundles were set on fire. Soon, the Shǔ camp was

CHINESE SAYINGS BOOK 3
EPISODE 18

ablaze, and the hot, dry weather, the east wind, and the forested setting, meant that the fire spread quickly westward, igniting other Shǔ military camps.

09:26 The Shǔ army was plunged into confusion, and the Wú forces gave chase. In fact, Wú forces had little to do but mop up after the fire as one Shǔ camp after another fell to the flames. Since Liú Bèi had spread his men over such a large territory, communications were sparse; but since all the camps were still technically connected, the fire could spread as it liked.

09:52 Sūn Huán, marveling at the success of Lù Xùn's plan, chose this time, when Liú Bèi could not possibly send reinforcements, to break the Shǔ siege at Yídào. The remains of Liú Bèi's army, retreating westwards, found their path blocked off by Sūn Huán.

10:11 After this turn of events, it was Liú Bèi, and not Sūn Quán, who was in a desperate position. Great generals of Shǔ had either lost their lives or been captured by Wú, not to mention the massive casualties and loss of equipment amongst the rest of the Shǔ army. Liú Bèi beat a sorry retreat to Báidì City 白帝城 in today's Chóngqìng where, weighed down by sorrows, he died the following year.

10:39 So this four character chengyu comes to us from this famous time of battles in Jīng Province, today's Húběi. Anyone, including yourself, who is willing to bite their tongue and suffer humiliation or abuse for the sake of laying low until it is the right time to strike, are Rěn Rǔ Fù Zhòng. Pleco explains it as enduring humiliation as part of an important mission. Our English equivalent might be to suffer in silence or suffer in silence for the sake of a higher objective.

11:15 Rěn Rǔ Fù Zhòng. That's our chengyu for this time.

11:19 Wow, the season is now half over. Can you believe it? Time flies when you're having fun doesn't it? Okay, that's all I got for you this time. Thanks for listening. This is Laszlo Montgomery signing off from our recording studios in Los Angeles, CA. Do consider joining me next time if you can, for another exciting episode of the Chinese Sayings Podcast.

Chinese Sayings Book 3 Episode 19

ALL I WANT IS TO BE NEXT TO YOU

近水楼台—Jìn Shuǐ Lóu Tái

TRANSCRIPT

00:00 | Greetings one and all, Laszlo Montgomery with you once again, another day another chéngyǔ. This is the Chinese Sayings Podcast now available on this very China History Podcast feed.

00:14 | And now for something completely different, a Chinese Saying that isn't from either the Zhou or Han Dynasty. Our story for this time comes straight out of the Southern Song Dynasty, 1127-1279.

00:28 | And we can thank a literary figure of the day who hailed from Lìshuǐ in Zhèjiāng province named Yú Wénbào 俞文豹 who wrote a collection of essays from a work called "Notes of a Clear Night", Qīng Yè Lù 清夜录. Yú Wénbào lived during the early 1200's during the time of the long reigning Sòng Emperor Lǐzōng 宋理宗. Scholars remember Yú Wénbào for his style of Chinese prose called Sǎnwén 散文. He wrote about local incidents and figures of the day and often exposed the corruption or failings within the Southern Song

CHINESE SAYINGS BOOK 3
EPISODE 19

	Dynasty's government.
01:05	During Yú Wénbào's time, the Sòng Dynasty was already on its last legs. And after Emperor Lǐzōng's dismal performance as ruler, reigning almost as long as the future do-nothing Míng Emperor Wànlì 明万历, the Sòng was easy meat for Kublai Khan's armies who toppled the dynasty in 1279.
01:26	And our saying is Jìn Shuǐ Lóu Tái 近水楼台. Four characters, as usual, standard for most all chéngyǔ, especially the ones with four characters. And let's break it down and move on to the story.
01:38	Jìn Shuǐ Lóu Tái.
01:40	Jìn 近 means be close to or to approach.
01:43	Shuǐ 水 is water. Jìnshuǐ 近水, near the water.
01:48	And a Lóutái 楼台 is a high building, a tower, pavilion or a balcony.
01:53	Strung together these four characters mean Near the water building or a building near the water. Easy enough. But what does this actually mean?
02:03	Let's not waste precious time sitting around trying to guess what that might mean. Let's go straight to the story which you may or may not be pleased to know is quite short. I'll have you on your way in no time.

CHINESE SAYINGS BOOK 3
EPISODE 19

02:15 | Top billing in this tale is the great Fàn Zhòngyān 范仲淹. He's been mentioned a few times in past CHP episodes. He's right up there with all the greatest scholars and thinkers of China going back to The Great Sage's time. And during the Northern Sòng in the first half of the 11th century, he was the biggest name there was, besides the emperor, and had served in most of the key roles in government.

02:42 | Fàn Zhòngyān was good at spotting talent and due to his own humble beginnings and modest circumstances, he took particular care to promote men who came from underprivileged backgrounds. During Fàn's period of service as a prefect in Hángzhōu 杭州, never did the government run smoother, so carefully had the officials been selected and placed in the most suitable position for each man. Fàn Zhòngyān had a long line of proteges, all grateful for his sponsorship and for giving them a chance to prove themselves in the government bureaucracy.

03:18 | But there was one man named Sū Lín 苏麟 who worked as a low-level official on the outskirts of Hángzhōu, in the suburbs, far from the center of action in the city. He was someone of ambition and like most aspiring men of his type he had high hopes to rise up in the bureaucracy.

03:34 | But time and time again, whenever promotions were made and officials were re-shuffled to other positions, he found himself passed over each and every time. Sū Lín took one look at his situation and knew, his failure to rise had nothing to do with his abilities. The problem

CHINESE SAYINGS BOOK 3
EPISODE 19

was he was too far away from Fàn Zhòngyān.

03:56 Fàn's office was located in the city center, a long distance from where Sū Lín was serving. If he had any hopes of going anywhere in the government he had to find a way to move closer to where the decisions were made. And that was wherever Fàn Zhòngyān was.

04:13 One day opportunity knocked. Like a bolt from the blue, Sū Lín was summoned to Fàn Zhòngyān's residence to deliver a report. And just like Salieri did for Mozart at Emperor Joseph II's palace when they met for the first time, Sū Lín prepared something special for the occasion. He composed a poem as a gift to Fàn Zhòngyān.

04:33 And it went: Jìnshuǐ lóutái xiāndé yuè, Xiàngyáng huāmù yìwéi chūn 近水楼台先得月，向阳花木易为春. And this translates to The waterside pavilion is the first to catch the moonlight, and the buds closest to the sun are the first to bloom in spring.

04:55 Now a literary figure of Fàn Zhòngyān's calibre was quick to figure out the meaning of this poem and the message Sū Lín was letting him know, subtly, through this poem and on this occasion. He used the term Jìnshuǐ lóutái, the waterside pavilion. It was jìnshuǐ, near to the water. In this poem the sun was Fàn Zhòngyān, and the jìnshuǐ lóutái is what Sū Lín aspired to be, near to the Fàn Zhòngyān so that his skills and proficiency would be noticed by the prefect. Without this Jìnshuǐ Lóutái, this waterside pavilion, close to where the action was, Su Lín knew he'd never get any shine and he'd forever

CHINESE SAYINGS BOOK 3
EPISODE 19

be stuck serving, unnoticed out in the sticks.

05:46 So from this poem Fàn Zhòngyān was most impressed and admitted his error in passing over Sū Lín for so long. After this, Sū Lín's career went nowhere but up.

05:57 So when you want to express your frustration about being so far from the action in your career, whether your cubicle is too distant from the boss or you rarely get any face time with the one person who could make it or break it for you, you need to get yourself a Jìnshuǐ lóutái.

06:14 This chéngyǔ has a couple versions. You can use the tried and true four character version, Jìnshuǐ Lóutái or you can add three more syllables and say Jìnshuǐ lóutái xiāndé yuè 近水楼台先得月. The waterside pavilion is the first to catch the moonlight. It means if one is in an advantageous position thanks to their closeness to the powers that be, then that person is most likely going to be the first one to obtain benefits from their proximity to the benefactor or boss.

06:46 Sometimes you may get lucky and fortune will smile on you as a matter of course. But if you're the type who doesn't like to sit around and wait for things to happen, you may need to find yourself a waterside pavilion to move into in order to be the first to catch that moonlight that can come in the form of a raise, a promotion, special recognition or stock options, who knows.

07:10 Jìnshuǐ lóutái. Special advantages comes to those in favorable positions. Once you are fortunate enough to obtain your own Jìnshuǐ lóutái, then you too can use your proximity to the powerful to obtain some benefit.

07:26 | Okay, let's call it a night and gather our things. This here's Laszlo Montgomery wishing you all my very best and inviting you to come back again next time, if you please, for another exciting episode of the Chinese Sayings Podcast.

Chinese Sayings Book 3 Episode 20

SHE'S A WOMAN

巾帼英雄—Jī Guó Yīng Xióng

TRANSCRIPT

00:00 | Welcome back my friends to the season that is coming to an end. Laszlo Montgomery here with the Chinese Sayings Podcast season seven closer. That was a quick twenty weeks if you ask me.

00:14 | And to finish things off, I bring you an old Chinese Saying that has multiple variations of a story that essentially involves a Jīnguó 巾帼, or a headscarf. And not just any headscarf.

00:27 | You recall perhaps the Yellow Turban and Red Turban Rebellions of the Eastern Han and Yuan Dynasties. The rebels wore these colored headscarves or turbans to identify themselves and from which their movement is remembered by.

00:44 | And from the same general time period of the Yellow Turban Rebellion of 184 to 205 AD, comes this story behind the Jīn Guó Yīng Xióng 巾帼英雄.

CHINESE SAYINGS BOOK 3
EPISODE 20

00:55 | A Jīn 巾 itself is a headscarf or towel or any kind of piece of cloth that could be worn by a man or a woman.

01:03 | And a Guó 帼 is also a scarf and the two words together, Jīnguó 巾帼, is used to describe a woman's headdress or silk scarf.

01:13 | And a yīngxióng 英雄 is a hero or heroine in this case. So these four characters that comprise two words literally means 'silk scarf hero'.

01:25 | Now, let's get to the story which comes to us courtesy of the the Book of Jìn 晋书, one of the twenty-four official histories of the dynasties, this one compiled by Táng dynasty historians who covered the years from around 170 AD in the Eastern Han to the fall of the Eastern Jìn and founding of the Liú Sòng in 420.

01:50 | And we have not one but two China history A-Listers headlining this tale. These are Zhūgě Liàng 诸葛亮 and Sīmǎ Yì 司马懿. Zhūgě Liàng of course the great military strategist and chancellor of the Shǔ Kingdom in China's southwest. And Sīmǎ Yì, grandfather to Jìn Dynasty founder Sīmǎ Yán 司马炎. Sīmǎ Yì, was Cao Cao's chancellor and go-to military leader for the Wèi State.

02:20 | During the Three Kingdoms period in the early 230's, Zhūgě Liàng once led a Shǔ 蜀国 army right up to the borders of the Kingdom of Wèi 魏国. However, their advance was halted by a strongly fortified Wèi encampment at Wèinán 渭南, an ancient city in modern-day Shǎnxī 陕西 and birthplace of Xí Zhòngxún 习仲勋.

CHINESE SAYINGS BOOK 3
EPISODE 20

That counts for something.

02:43 And this fortified encampment was commanded by the Wèi general Sīmǎ Yì. Try as he might there was no way for Zhūgě Liàng's army to advance further into Wèi unless they were able to get past Sīmǎ Yì's army first. However, the military advantages in this standoff were squarely on the side of Sīmǎ Yì.

03:06 The Wèi encampment was so well defended and supplied that if they wanted to, they could comfortably survive the siege for months to come. And the invading Shǔ army, this far north, was far from their Sichuan home and camped out within enemy territory.

03:25 It had already been a huge drain on Shǔ's time, manpower, and money to get their forces this far, and it woulda been a pity for them to turn tail and head back to Shǔ now. Thus, Zhūgě Liàng's goal was to break the siege on Wèinán quickly, before morale and supplies ran out.

03:44 To this end, Zhūgě Liàng sent his soldiers multiple times a day to taunt Sīmǎ Yì. The Shǔ soldiers hurled the most degrading insults and humiliating taunts imaginable at the Wèi encampment, but Sīmǎ Yì kept the Wèi forces at bay and refused to let them engage the Shǔ army.

04:08 Almost at his wits end, Zhūgě Liàng came up with one final plan. He sent a Shǔ delegation to to the Wèi encampment with a 'gift' for Sīmǎ Yì. When Sīmǎ Yì opened the large, richly wrapped package, out tumbled a cascade of women's hair ornaments and silken headscarves or jīnguó. Zhūgě Liàng's intention was to scoff at their cowardice and imply that their soldiers were no better than a bunch of women who, back then, usually didn't enlist in the military.

04:43 Of all Zhūgě Liàng's ploys, this was the one that came the closest to working. Sīmǎ Yì and his forces were absolutely furious at this insult. However, at the very last moment, Sīmǎ Yì reflected that, no matter how brazen a taunt Zhūgě Liàng had sent, it would be unspeakably rash to engage the Shǔ forces in the open when the Wèi army was so advantageously protected in their encampment. Swallowing his anger, he once again gave orders that the Wèi army was to remain in place.

05:17 In some versions of the story, Sīmǎ Yì even put on the silk scarf and hair ornaments sent to him by Zhūgě Liàng, and paraded in front of the Shǔ messengers dressed in women's clothing to show that he was not bothered by Zhūgě Liàng's insinuation.

05:34 Either way, Sīmǎ Yì's refusal to allow a taunt to his masculinity to lure him into rash action saved the Wèi army on that occasion. And not that long afterwards in 234, Zhūgě Liàng passed away after five unsuccessful tries to take down the State of Wèi.

05:54 And later, the phrase 'silk scarf' or jīnguó became an honorific reserved for women. And the term Jīnguó Yīngxióng or 'silk scarf hero' became widely used to refer to those women who displayed no less bravery and

CHINESE SAYINGS BOOK 3
EPISODE 20

military aptitude than their male counterparts.

06:14 A few famous 'silk scarf heroes' from Chinese history and literature included Empress Wǔ Zétiān 武则天, the Shang dynasty general, priestess and queen consort Lady Fùhǎo 妇好, the legendary woman warrior Mùlán 花木兰 and the revolutionary and feminist great from the late 19th-early 20th century, Qiū Jǐn 秋瑾. All were considered Jīnguó Yīngxióng.

06:39 So you can describe any heroic or brave or strong woman who stands up and doesn't take any you know what from anyone, a Jīnguó Yīngxióng. They need not be brave in battle. It can be used for any female who stands up for herself or who overcomes any obstacles in her way and shows courage and steely determination in everything she does, especially in the face of adversity or discrimination. No matter defending her nation, her community, her family or herself, a woman who doesn't crack under pressure and achieves in the face of adversity, that's a Jīnguó Yīngxiōng.

07:22 There's no shortage of stories of women heroes in China associated with the chéngyǔ Jīnguó Yīngxiōng.

07:29 In modern times, Jīn Guó Yīng Xióng can also refer to women who have made outstanding contributions in various fields, such as science, politics, sports, or the arts. The term is often used as a way to recognize and celebrate the achievements of women and to inspire others to follow in their footsteps.

CHINESE SAYINGS BOOK 3
EPISODE 20

07:51 And that is gonna be it. Okay, enough of this tittle-tattle. As I do every time at the end of each CSP season, I'm gonna take a bit of a break and you can rest assured I'll be back with more fabulous and useful Chinese Sayings. And so many of you over the years have told me you've been able to convey the essence of your entire point or message using just a few of these sayings that you picked up from listening to this program. Really, why ramble on and on about something when four Chinese characters will say the same thing for ya.

08:25 Okay, my deepest thanks, as always. This here's Laszlo Montgomery signing off from Jiāzhōu Luòshānjī 加州洛杉矶 thanking you once more with feeling, and cordially inviting you to come back next time for another exciting episode of the Chinese Sayings Podcast.

 Chinese Sayings Book 3
Episode 21

THE TRANSCRIPTS

BLUE, BLUE, MY WORLD IS BLUE

青出于蓝—Qīng Chū Yú Lán

TRANSCRIPT

00:00 Welcome back, ladies and gentlemans, to the Chinese Sayings Podcast. Laszlo Montgomery here with you, presenting a new chengyu for your ever-expanding collezione. Last week ran a little longer than the usual CSP fare so this time I'll have you outta here much quicker.

00:20 This was another early one I picked up during the first year of Chinese study: Qīng Chū Yú Lán 青出于蓝. I didn't know it way back then but we have Xúnzǐ 荀子 to thank for this one. Xúnzǐ of course, was the philosopher who parted ways with the great Méngzǐ 孟子 and postulated that human nature was fundamentally evil. But the great Master Xún, he said evil by nature though it may be, humankind had it in their power to constantly strive to better itself through ceaseless personal cultivation and education.

00:56 And this Chinese Saying, Qīng Chū Yú Lán, comes from the chapter Encouraging Learning. Quànxué 劝

CHINESE SAYINGS BOOK 3
EPISODE 21

	学, from Xúnzǐ's thirty-two-chapter philosophical work, the Xúnzǐ. And this tale testifies to his belief in the possibility, necessity, and value of constant education and learning to improve oneself.
01:20	Let's break down the characters. This one actually has a rejoinder to it but in this episode I'll only make you remember the essential first four.
01:30	Qīng 青, as an adjective means a special kind of blue or greenish blue color.
01:35	Chūyú 出于 means out of or from.
01:39	And Lán 蓝 means blue or in this case indigo blue, which is very dark. Blue or blue-green or simply bright blue from dark blue. In so many words.
01:51	The idiom first came from Xúnzǐ but it was quoted throughout the centuries, perhaps most famously with respect to a story concerning the disciple of a famous scholar of the Northern and Southern Dynasties Period named Kǒng Fán 孔璠.
02:07	He had a loyal disciple, named Lǐ Mì 李谧, who was a hardworking and conscientious young scholar, and quickly became one of Kǒng Fán's favorite students. Kǒng Fán painstaking taught Lǐ Mì everything he knew, and Lǐ Mì was so good at his studies that in a few years, his knowledge and erudition surpassed his teacher, Kǒng Fán.

CHINESE SAYINGS BOOK 3
EPISODE 21

02:29 However, the thing about Lǐ Mì was that, as brilliant as he may have been, he was also a humble student, and he refused to do anything that might be construed as showing off his superior knowledge in front of anyone, especially Master Kǒng Fán.

02:44 Kǒng Fán had a habit of discussing complex problems with his students, and he was not above asking his students for opinions and pointing to his shortcomings when he didn't have the answer. One day during a seminar, Kǒng Fán asked Lǐ Mì a difficult question, one that he, the teacher, did not know how to answer. Lǐ Mì knew the answer, but he didn't want to appear more knowledgeable than his teacher and flex in front of everyone with his answers. He merely stammered out a perfunctory reply to Kǒng Fán's direct question.

03:22 After the seminar was over, Kǒng Fán asked Lǐ Mì to stay behind and called him into his study. Kǒng Fán said, "When I ask you a question, please do not hesitate to reply out of consideration for my status as your teacher. Did Confucius himself not say, Sān rén xíng, bì yǒu wǒ shī 三人行必有我师 "Out of every three men, at least one can teach me something"? It is an honour to learn from anyone who knows more about any subject than I do. And from a young man like you, who is more knowledgeable than I am about so many things, how much I could learn if you would only teach me!"

04:00 Someone must have overheard the exchange between teacher and student, because when word got out about this incident of Kǒng Fán asking his student to become

CHINESE SAYINGS BOOK 3
EPISODE 21

his teacher, it caused a great stir in the intellectual and literati communities of the time.

04:15 It was considered by all, a double win. First they praised Kǒng Fán's humble spirit as a teacher, and his love of learning for the sake of learning, and never acting pretentious about his scholarship. And Lǐ Mì too. He was praised for his respectful nature, and sharing his teacher's commitment to knowledge and learning, and placing degrees and status as unimportant.

04:40 These colleagues of Lǐ Mì harkening back to those four characters from the Xùnzǐ, composed a popular song about this incident that went: "Indigo is made from blue; blue gives way to indigo. Qīng chéng lán, lán xiè qīng. Shī hécháng, zài míng jīng 青成蓝，蓝谢青。师何尝，在明经. The student who knows better becomes the teacher."

05:04 So, Indigo comes from blue, and yet surpasses blue. A student's talents may exceed the master's from whom he learns. This one is perfect for situations to describe any instance in which the student surpasses their teacher. Or the one being taught is more skillful that the one doing the teaching.

05:24 And this is in no way limited to students and teachers. This can also be colleagues at work, in sports, in music, or the arts. It can even refer to the present exceeding the past, although nowadays I'm beginning to wonder.

05:37 So once again Qīng Chū Yú Lán. Two takeaways. No

CHINESE SAYINGS BOOK 3
EPISODE 21

one will diminish their standing or face by asking a question of those who know better than them, no matter whether they are younger, a student, a junior colleague or someone you recognize who knows more than you do. And the second takeaway, all you brilliant minds, remember Lǐ Mì and his humility despite his great abilities as a scholar. You wouldn't see him tweeting about how smart and witty he was or posting calling attention to himself on social media.

06:11 That's the fate of many a teacher wherever they are in this world. No matter their brilliance or effectiveness at teaching, there are always pupils whose innate brilliance will allow them to transcend the teaching of the teacher. Like Matt Damon's character in Good Will Hunting or Obi Wan Kenobi and Qui Gon Jinn.

06:31 Leonardo da Vinci once said, "Poor is the teacher whose student does not surpass him." So, keep all that in mind all you teachers, professors, mentors and geniuses. The more students who surpass you in learning and achievement, the better a teacher you were.

06:47 I told you this one was gonna be short. Qīng Chū Yú Lán. And the rejoinder I told you about. It goes like this: qīng chū yú lán ér shèng yú lán 青出于蓝, 而胜于蓝 which just says bright blue comes from blue and even surpasses lán 蓝 or this indigo blue. Like I said, Qīng Chūyú Lán will get you through any situation.

07:09 So that's gonna be it, mes amis. This is Laszlo Montgomery signing off from LA on a hot day in July,

CHINESE SAYINGS BOOK 3
EPISODE 21

in the Year of the Cat. My favorite year. Please consider coming back next time for another useful episode of the Chinese Sayings Podcast.

Chinese Sayings Book 3
Episode 22

SHOCK THE MONKEY

树倒猢狲散—Shù Dǎo Hú Sūn Sàn

TRANSCRIPT

00:00	Greetings good people, all over the world, this is Laszlo Montgomery bringing you another Chinese Saying here at the podcast show that, since 2016, has, even to this day, remained true to its name, The Chinese Sayings Podcast.
00:18	Today's featured chengyu, for a change, doesn't come from the Spring and Autumn or Warring States periods. Our selection for this time comes from a mostly forgotten figure, a scholar official from the Northern Sòng Dynasty named Páng Yuányīng 庞元英. He wrote a collection of essays on diverse topics called Tán Sǒu 谈薮, or Congregating to Hold Conversation.
00:41	And the featured chengyu that we're going to examine today goes like this: Shù Dǎo Húsūn Sàn 树倒猢狲散.
00:50	But before we jump to the story, here's a quick analysis of the five characters that make up this chengyu.

163

CHINESE SAYINGS BOOK 3
EPISODE 22

00:56 | A shù 树 is a tree.

00:58 | And the character dǎo 倒 in the third tone, means to fall. Shùdǎo 树倒, a tree falls.

01:06 | A Húsūn 猢狲 is a monkey or specifically a macaque.

01:11 | And the last character sàn 散 means to scatter or disburse.

01:15 | Shù Dǎo Húsūn Sàn. Tree falls monkeys scatter.

01:21 | Without knowing the story you may be able to guess the meaning behind this one. But if you've never heard the story behind these five characters, you're left to guess what's the backstory behind Shù Dǎo Húsūn Sàn.

01:35 | And the lead character of our story is one of the all-time great villains from Chinese history and certainly from the times he lived in. And this was Qín Huì 秦桧. If there was one person from Chinese history who has been spat on more than Qín Huì, I don't know who that night be. More about that in a bit. Qín Huì was a high ranking official at the court of the ill-fated Sòng Emperors Huīzōng 宋徽宗, and Qīnzōng 宋钦宗. All of this was covered ad nauseam in the CHP four-part series covering the life of Emperor Huīzōng. That was CHP episodes 132 to 135.

02:14 | By the year 1126, the Jürchens, who had already established the Jīn 金 Dynasty in Northern China, began pushing closer to the Northern Song capital of Biànjīng 汴京, which is modern-day Kāifēng 开封, Hénán province.

CHINESE SAYINGS BOOK 3
EPISODE 22

02:31 | These Jürchens were a warlike tribal confederation with very strong leadership. Their homelands were in the cold northeast of China. We remember them today as the Manchus. But back in the 12th Century they were known as the Jürchens. They had been probing Sòng China from the north and figured out that the defenses were in no state to resist if they chose to mount a full-scale invasion. The Jürchens, assured of their military superiority, were not afraid to become more aggressive and pushy with the demands they kept making with the Song royal court.

03:09 | One day, the Jürchen ruler dispatched an envoy to the Sòng imperial court telling them, if they only handed over these three towns, they'd no longer make any further incursions into Sòng territory.

03:23 | Facing this grave challenge, Qín Huì strongly insisted that the Sòng should not show any weakness in the face of this oncoming Jürchen's invasion. He wrote multiple memorials to the Emperor, essentially arguing that if the Sòng were to grant the Jürchen's these three towns, the Jürchens would know at once the Sòng were in sad shape and the demands would never cease. But Qín Huì's requests were overruled and the three towns were indeed granted to the Jürchens. And just as Qín Huì had predicted, in 1127, the Jürchens besieged, and then captured, the Sòng imperial capital itself.

04:06 | And in one of the most humiliating episodes in the history of imperial China the Jürchens took as their prisoners, the Emperor Qīnzōng, his father, the former

Emperor Huīzōng, a considerable retinue of Northern Sòng officials, including Qín Huì and almost the entire royal family. And they were all sent on a forced march to one of the coldest most inhospitable parts of Hēilóngjiāng in Manchuria to live out the rest of their lives. Emperor Huīzōng died in 1135 and his son, Emperor Qīnzōng, he lasted until 1161.

04:45 Qín Huì was also among the prisoners taken by the Jürchens. But he survived the ordeal and surprisingly, even though he previously maintained a militant stance against the Jürchens, he knew who buttered his bread and ingratiated himself with his captors.

05:04 They had gotten to know Qín Huì after he had been called upon by Huīzōng to write and present a letter of surrender to the Jürchens. In this document, the Emperor offered the Jürchens heavy bribes as well as a promise to act as their vassal state if the Jürchens would only let him return south to his homeland.

05:23 The Jürchens didn't accept this proposal, but they looked very kindly on its writer and messenger, Qín Huì. From then on, Qín Huì found himself well-treated by the Jürchen royals. In his capacity as a former Song court official and advisor, he was often passed around the households of important Jürchens as a gift. From the years 1127-1130, he even rode out on a series of battles with Jürchen leaders bent on conquering even more Sòng territory. He had clearly gone over to the other side.

CHINESE SAYINGS BOOK 3
EPISODE 22

06:00 | In 1130, acting on some mysterious motive, Qín Huì escaped from the Jürchens and one day reappeared at the Southern Sòng court. The Sòng Dynasty, its previous territorial holdings considerably shrunken, was now ruled by another of Emperor Huīzōng's sons, Emperor Gāozōng who had moved the Sòng capital south, to Jīnlíng 金陵, modern-day Nanjing on the other side of the Yangzi River, just out of reach of the Jürchens.

06:32 | At the new Sòng capital and under a new Emperor, Qín Huì gave them a whole song and dance about how he had killed his Jürchen guards and made this daring escape. The new Emperor, glad to regain an experienced official from his father's court, didn't ask too many questions, and Qín Huì was reincorporated into the Sòng dynasty ranks.

06:54 | Contrary to his old stance against the Jürchens, in 1141 Qín Huì was instrumental in brokering a peace treaty between the Southern Sòng and the Jürchen Jīn Dynasty. This was the Treaty of Shàoxīng 绍兴, where the Southern Sòng effectively agreed to become a tribute nation to the Jürchens, and also agreed to give up claims to contested territory in the north of China.

07:21 | Although this treaty meant that the Jürchens left the Southern Sòng mostly in peace for another decade, it came at a high cost. For one thing, there was the popular and talented Sòng general Yuè Fēi 岳飞. Yuè Fēi was known for his extreme patriotism and his willingness to fight the Jürchens for every inch of Sòng territory. And he did not agree with the words contained in this

Shàoxīng Treaty. And so popular and influential was Yuè Fēi, his resistance to giving in to Jūrchen demands became widespread and shared by the people. Therefore in order to remove Yuè Fēi from the equation, Qín Huì hatched a plot to have him executed before the Emperor could intercede on his behalf.

08:09 I detailed the tragic death of Yuè Fēi in CHP episode 95. This great hero in Chinese history was executed at the hands of the dynasty to whom he had been loyal all his life. And in the process, by dying tragically, he turned Qín Huì into a popular villain in the eyes of history.

08:30 Perhaps Qín Huì truly had the Sòng Dynasty's best interests at heart when he brokered the Treaty of Shàoxīng. But in doing so, he pitted his reputation against one of China's best-loved popular figures. As folktales about Yuè Fēi's courage, patriotism, and conviction spread in every successive dynasty, so did folktales about Qín Huì's duplicity, smallness of mind, and weakness.

08:58 One such popular tale is the tale of Cáo Yǒng 曹咏, one of Qín Huì's loyal followers when Qín returned to the Southern court and began gaining power. As the story goes, Cáo Yǒng earned a high position in the Sòng court by sucking up to and flattering Qín Huì. Because of his closeness to Qín Huì, Cáo Yǒng grew rich and powerful, and all his friends and relatives began cozying up to him now that he had newfound wealth and power.

CHINESE SAYINGS BOOK 3
EPISODE 22

09:29 | But there was one relative who refused to do so. And that was his wife's brother, Lì Désī 历德斯. Lì Désī not only refused to be friendly with Cáo Yǒng, but he actually criticized him to his face and also behind his back, saying: "This husband of my sister has no real talent. He only got to where he is by virtue of sucking up to Qín Huì."

09:56 | The relationship between the two men was, understandably, strained, and they spent much of their life sparring politically, trying to take each other down. When Qín Huì was alive and in favour, Cáo Yǒng was untouchable; however, after Qín Huì died in 1155, the Emperor Gāozōng demoted many of Qín Huì's former cronies. Cáo Yǒng was no exception.

10:19 | As the now disgraced and demoted Cáo and his family travelled, with their tail between their legs, to take up a new post in one of the provinces, a fast messenger arrived with a letter from Lì Désī. And this is where we get the chengyu.

10:35 | When Cáo Yǒng opened the letter, it contained a mocking poem Lì Désī had written. The poem contained the following couplet from which we get this Chinese Saying:

10:46 | Huā Kāi Dié Mǎn Zhī, Shù Dǎo Hú sūn Sàn—花开蝶满枝, 树倒猢狲散. When the blossoms bloom, butterflies fill the branches; When the great tree falls, the monkeys scatter.

10:59 | The poem made Cáo Yǒng so comically angry that he tore it to pieces while gnashing his teeth; but, of course, he was now in no position to do anything in retaliation.

11:10 | This poem was pretty clear in its meaning. When someone's in power or riding high due to circumstances, they will have no shortage of followers. Everybody's trying to be their baby. But as soon as they fall from power or their luck runs out, their followers unfollow them and scatter. The last part of this phrase is used derogatorily to describe people who leave opportunistically when their leader falls.

11:39 | This is sort of like that chengyu from Season 4, Mén Kě Luó Què 门可罗雀. That one featured Hàn Dynasty figure Lord Zhái, once so popular his courtyard was filled with hangers on. But as soon as he fell from power, you could catch sparrows in a net in his courtyard, so few were the guests calling on him. I'm sure all cultures have something similar to this tale. Nobody loves you when you're down and out, just like John sang on the Walls and Bridges album.

12:08 | So, that's the story behind Shù Dǎo Hú Sūn Sàn. When the tree falls, the monkeys scatter. That's sort of a distant cousin to rats deserting the sinking ship.

12:20 | And you get extra credit if you say the five characters that precede our Chinese Saying for this episode, Huā Kāi Dié Mǎn Zhī. When the blossoms bloom, butterflies fill the branches. But in real life, when you use this chengyu, all you need to say is Shù Dǎo Hú Sūn Sàn. A

CHINESE SAYINGS BOOK 3
EPISODE 22

regular occurrence in politics.

12:41 And as far as Qín Huì getting spit on, if you go to the Yuè Fēi Temple in Hangzhou they have iron statues inside the courtyard of Qín Huì and his wife who was just like him. And although you can't do this any more, over the years people would go there and spit on these two iron statues. And there's now a sign there saying "Don't Spit on the Statues". So, if you ever go to Hangzhou, visit the Yue Fei Temple and don't spit on Qín Huì and his wife, but take in the whole scene and remember this chengyu, Shù Dǎo Hú sūn Sàn.

13:18 Okay, that's gonna be it for this time. I thank you all kindly for stopping by and listening. We're now halfway through Season 8. Time sure does fly when you're having fun.

13:28 All right, as always, this is your host and humble narrator Laszlo Montgomery signing off from Santa Monica, California this time. But you probably couldn't tell. Please please me, oh yeah, and consider the possibility of joining me next time for another useful episode of the Chinese Sayings Podcast.

 Chinese Sayings Book 3
Episode 23

DON'T COUNT ME OUT YET

大器晚成—Dà Qì Wǎn Chéng

TRANSCRIPT

00:00 | Good afternoon everyone all around this beautiful world, Laszlo Montgomery with you as always with another Chinese Sayings Podcast episode. Hard to believe this season is already coming to a glorious end.

00:16 | And for the fourth time at least since we began this family program back in 2016, we snagged another one from the Sān Guó Zhì 三国志, the Record of the Three Kingdoms. This great classic from antiquity covers those years of the fall of the Eastern Han clear through to the Three Kingdoms Period. We have Chén Shòu 陈寿 to thank for this text that he compiled in the Jìn 晋朝 following reunification of the country.

00:41 | And before we hear the story from this text taken from the Record of Wèi 三国志-魏志, let's break down the four characters that make up this chéngyǔ.

00:50 | Dà Qì Wǎn Chéng 大器晚成.

CHINESE SAYINGS BOOK 3
EPISODE 23

00:54 — Dà 大 means big or great.

00:56 — And qì 器 means a utensil of some sort but in the case of this chengyu, it means capacity or talent. And Dàqì 大器 together means men of great talent or capable people.

01:09 — Wǎn 晚 means late and chéng 成 means means accomplish or succeed or to become or turn into.

01:15 — And when you line it all up we get men of great talent late turn into.

01:21 — Well, I guess we can figure out where this one is going. But let's get to the story already and find out who this Chinese Saying is referring to.

01:30 — We're back in the waning years of the Eastern Han Dynasty. So it's a given that the Cáo Family will figure prominently in our story. Cáo Cāo 曹操 and his sons Cáo Pī 曹丕 and Cáo Zhí 曹植 are characters in this tale.

01:44 — But the star of our episode is someone who served the Cáo Family. And his name was Cuī Yǎn 崔琰. He was a famous swordsman who later became a learned scholar and a trusted advisor of Cáo Cāo. He was born into a very honored and esteemed family from the Qīnghé Commandery 清河郡, one of the thirty-six that were established in the Qín Dynasty. Qīnghé was located in southern Héběi and western Shāndōng. The Cuī Family would later rise to even greater prominence during the 6th and 7th centuries.

CHINESE SAYINGS BOOK 3
EPISODE 23

02:20 | But in his early years Cuī Yǎn was renowned for his skills handling a sword. His excellent swordplay allowed him to travel far and wide and make many friends. But as Cuī Yǎn's fame spread and people fawned all over him like the sports athletes in our day, the word began to get out that although he was a brilliant swordsman, he wasn't much of a man of learning and had no interest in studying or knowledge.

02:51 | One day, Cuī Yǎn went to call on someone who was respected as a noted scholar. When the man's servant answered the door and Cuī Yǎn introduced himself, the servant told him to wait outside while he announced Cuī Yǎn to his master. Not five minutes had passed when the servant came back to Cuī Yǎn and said, "My master says he is too busy with his studies to spend time on trivial matters."

03:18 | Upon hearing this Cuī Yǎn was deeply ashamed and downright humiliated. He understood this message to mean that even though he was a well-known swordsman, the scholar thought there was nothing to gain by inviting him into his study for a conversation. Beyond his handiness with a sword, he was someone of little substance and had no knowledge of the world. After taking in this bitter pill, Cuī Yǎn secretly resolved that from then on, he would study as hard as he could until he became someone renowned both for his scholarship and his swordplay.

03:56 | True to his resolve, Cuī Yǎn spent years studying, until he too became noted for his knowledge, wisdom, and strategy. So famous and renowned did he become, he was hired as one of the advisors of the famous warlord, Cáo Cāo, who had rose to become the de facto head of the Hàn Dynasty.

04:15 In Cáo Cāos military base Yèchéng 邺城, in today's southern Hebei Province near present-day Hándān, Cuī Yǎn quickly rose through the ranks and became one of Cáo Cāo's favorite strategists.

04:29 Indeed, Cáo Cāo valued Cuī Yǎn's opinion so much that the day came when he asked Cuī Yǎn which of his sons he should make heir to his considerable territories. Cáo Cāo had already been granted the title of a vassal king by Hàn Emperor Xiàn and ruled the autonomous kingdom of Wèi, which was nominally still under the Han dynasty.

04:52 Cuī Yǎn gave this advice to Cáo Cāo: "Sir, I know you wish to make your youngest son, Cáo Zhí, heir to your position. But since ancient times, there has been a Confucian tradition of giving precedence to eldest sons. If you break this tradition, your court ministers will be surprised and unsettled. Even worse than that, your eldest son Cáo Pī may begin to have mutinous thoughts. Thus, you will have planted the seeds of your own dynasty's destruction. I beg you to turn your eyes upon history. Has it ever ended well when a father has passed over an elder brother for a younger one?"

05:34 Cáo Cāo was extremely pleased with this advice. This was because he knew that Cuī Yǎn was speaking in an

CHINESE SAYINGS BOOK 3
EPISODE 23

unbiased manner and strictly following the Confucian tradition. Cuī Yǎn's own interest was with Cáo Zhí, since he was related to Cáo Zhí through his mother. Yet, despite this, Cuī Yǎn had still recommended Cáo Pī for succession over Cáo Zhí. From then on, Cáo Cāo respected Cuī Yǎn even more for his fair-mindedness, later promoting him to the high position of Zhōngwèi 中尉, Commandant of the Capital. A zhōngwèi in today's military ranking is akin to a first lieutenant.

06:12 Cuī Yǎn had a young kinsman named Cuī Lín 崔林. Cuī Lín was a dissolute youth and a borderline wastrel who was not at all well regarded by his fellow Cuī Family relatives. They had looked down on him as the family ne'er-do-well who would never amount to anything. Only Cuī Yǎn saw him in a different light.

06:34 After Cuī Yǎn had risen to such great heights in Cáo Cāo's Wèi Kingdom, becoming a powerful and well-respected military advisor, he remembered his own younger days, when he had done nothing except roam around practicing with his sword. It had taken him a while to shake off his past and work hard to attain a modicum of greatness in the government.

06:58 He therefore said to anyone who would listen, "The greater the latent potential someone has, the longer it will take for this potential to manifest itself. Don't dismiss Cuī Lín. I'm sure he will eventually become someone extraordinary."

07:13 Here Cuī Yǎn uttered our featured chengyu for this

CHINESE SAYINGS BOOK 3
EPISODE 23

episode when he mentioned that Cuī Lín was a clear case of Dàqì Wǎnchéng. That contrary to what his Cuī relatives thought, Cuī Lín would later in life become someone of importance and value to the state. And true to Cuī Yǎn's prediction, indeed Cuī Lín did eventually became a high-ranking official, faithfully serving the Kingdom of Cáo Wèi in a number of important positions until the end of his days.

07:45 So his family didn't think much of his prospects but Cuī Yǎn, looking at his own life experience, knew that his young relative Cuī Lín was a case of Dàqì Wǎnchéng and that his great talent would one day, later on, manifest itself.

08:04 That's the way it is sometimes. Dàqì Wǎnchéng. Some of us don't really reveal their greatness or peak in their careers till much later in life. He didn't work in government, but Ray Kroc was a case of Dàqì Wǎnchéng. He didn't turn McDonald's into the fast food empire it became until he was well into his fifties. And you can say the same thing about Colonel Harland Sanders of KFC, Nelson Mandela, Winston Churchill, Angela Merkel. They too were examples of Dàqì Wǎnchéng. They didn't shine on the world stage until well into their fifties.

08:44 So this is a good chengyu to keep handy whenever you want to describe someone who, maybe in their younger days didn't amount to much, but who one day would achieve greatness in whatever it was they sought out to do. This could be in politics, sports, commerce, science and engineering or anything, even literary endeavors.

CHINESE SAYINGS BOOK 3
EPISODE 23

Dà Qì Wǎn Chéng.

09:07 Let me just close with a quick follow-up to the life of Cuī Yǎn. In 216 AD, Cui Yan got himself caught up in some political skullduggery and was accused of defaming Cao Cao in a letter. Though innocent of these charges, he ended up being stripped of his high ranking position and tossed into prison where he was forced to commit suicide. Yeah, those years just before the fall of the Hàn, not for the squeamish.

09:35 Thanks for listening and I'll see you again next time in season 10 for another satisfying lineup of chengyu's at the Chinese Sayings Podcast.

Chinese Sayings Book 3
Episode 24

THE TRUTH ALWAYS GETS OUT

东窗事发—Dōng Chuāng Shì Fā

TRANSCRIPT

00:00	Greetings all CHP listeners all over the world. Laszlo Montgomery here with the Season 9 opener.
00:09	Starring in today's chéngyǔ story is the very same Yuè Fēi 岳飞 and Qín Huì 秦桧 who we featured last season in the chengyu Shù Dǎo Húsūn Sàn 树倒猢狲散. Who can forget that one? Well, Qín Huì is back. Today we give the Chinese Saying Dōng chuāng Shì Fā 东窗事发 a once-over.
00:28	Dōng Chuāng Shì Fā. What does that literally mean?
00:32	Dōng 东 is east and chuāng 窗 is a window.
00:35	Shì 事 means matter or affair, thing or business.
00:40	And fā 发 in this usage means exposed or to get out.
00:46	East Window matter exposed. I'll be truthful with you. Not unless you're already quite familiar with the story

CHINESE SAYINGS BOOK 3
EPISODE 24

of the demise of Yuè Fēi can you even begin to know what this one might be all about.

00:59　If by chance you're already well versed in the Yuán Dynasty work Qiántáng Yíshì 钱塘遗事 by Liú Yìqīng 刘一清, this story might be old hat to you. This text, Assorted Matters of Qiántáng concerned various historical stories from Liú Yìqīng's part of Hangzhou known as Qiántáng, named after the great river, of course. His stories concerned various affairs that went down during the Southern Song when Hangzhou was where the capital was located.

01:30　As you recall the Song Dynasty was delivered a walloping knockout punch by the Jürchens and their Jīn Dynasty. One of the royal's, Zhào Gòu 赵构 escaped and went on to re-establish the dynasty on the other side of the Yangtze River in Hangzhou. He reigned as Sòng Emperor Gāozōng. His father of course was emperor Huīzōng.

01:53　And despite all that had happened, Yuè Fēi fought on against the Jürchens and wouldn't give up until he pushed them back north into their lands. Qín Huì, who served as chancellor, had spent some time as a captive of the Jürchens once, was eager to appease them and get them to tone down their aggression against the reconstituted Song Dynasty.

02:17　Yuè Fēi was immensely popular with the people and was regarded as a hero for taking the fight to China's Jürchen tormenters. But Qín Huì wished to get rid of Yuè Fēi,

CHINESE SAYINGS BOOK 3
EPISODE 24

who had become a stone in his boot for too long now.

02:33 One night he whispered quietly with his wife, Lady Wáng 王氏, in a private room in their house. They stood next to a window that faced east. There was no one present to overhear their conspiratorial exchange of words. But Qín Huì and his wife, since the matter was top secret and of utmost importance, made sure they were alone. Yuè Fēi was extremely popular with the people and if there was the slightest suspicion of foul play, Qín Huì would suffer dire political consequences.

03:06 Despite his misgivings, Lady Wáng urged her husband Qín Huì to get rid of Yuè Fēi once and for all. She said to him, Zhuō hǔ róngyì, fàng hǔ jiù nánle 捉虎容易，放虎就难了！"It is easier to catch a tiger than to deal with him once he has escaped."

03:22 Qín Huì saw that his wife's advice was convincing enough. And so he decided to act quickly to kill Yuè Fēi. But to execute such a popular figure, he needed criminal charges that were absolutely ironclad, preferably from an insider in Yuè Fēi's own camp. Lady Wáng said, "I know there is a general in Yuè Fēi's army, Wáng Guì 王贵, who turned and ran during a battle, and who Yuè Fēi had whipped as punishment. Surely, to seek revenge against Yuè Fēi, Wáng Guì will be happy to provide the evidence we need."

04:00 The next day, Qín Huì had Wáng Guì arrested and brought to him. When Wáng Guì proved unwilling to betray Yuè Fēi, Qín Huì had him tortured and beaten

CHINESE SAYINGS BOOK 3
EPISODE 24

until he finally gave him the confession he was looking for. Based on these flimsy and trumped-up charges, Qín Huì thereupon had Yuè Fēi arrested and soon after, on January 28, 1142, had him executed for treason.

04:30 Not long after, Qín Huì was enjoying a pleasure cruise upon the beautiful West Lake, in Hangzhou, when he suddenly started feeling feverish and unwell. In the midst of his fever, suddenly appearing before his eyes was the ghost of an unkempt man, with long hair hanging loose and wild all over his face, standing in the middle of the boat.

04:55 Qín Huì recoiled in utter terror when suddenly this man pointed an accusing finger at him and cried out in a thunderous voice, "You have destroyed the nation and failed the people. I have told Heaven what you plotted, and soon you will have to answer for your crimes against Heaven!" After saying this, as quickly as he had appeared, the man vanished into thin air.

05:21 Qín Huì died soon after this in 1155, and on the heels of his passing, his son, Qín Xī 秦熺 died also. Lady Wáng, distraught and grieving at the double loss of her husband and son, contacted a Taoist priest who supposedly had the ability to communicate with spirits in the afterlife.

05:41 Prior to the meeting with Lady Wáng, the priest carried out all the requisite sacrifices and rituals. Then he began the ceremony and soon began his communion with Lady Wáng's husband, the former chancellor Qín Huì. As soon as he accessed the afterlife, the priest saw

CHINESE SAYINGS BOOK 3
EPISODE 24

Qín Huì's son, Qín Xī, weighed down with chains and manacles. He asked Qín Xī, "Where is your father?" Qín Xī said, "You will find him in the capital city of the Underworld."

06:16 The priest left Qín Huì's son to his torture and agony and journeyed to the capital of the Underworld. Upon his arrival, he saw Qín Huì who was even more chained and manacled than his son. He was being tortured and manhandled by a group of devils as his eternal punishment. Qín Huì espied the spirit of the Taoist priest. His eyes locked on the priest's and Qín Huì pleaded with him, "I beg you to tell my wife: Dōng Chuāng Shì Fā. The plot at the East Window has been discovered after all! Dōng Chuāng Shì Fā. That matter they privately and surreptitiously discussed next to the east window, where they thought they'd be alone in their residence, had gotten out.

07:04 Whenever you wish to describe a nefarious plot or scheme that comes to light despite every attempt made to keep it a secret, you can say those four syllables, Dōng Chuāng Shì Fā. As Benjamin Franklin once said, three can keep a secret if two of them are dead. The truth always finds a way of percolating to the surface.

07:27 Those with guilty consciences will be tormented by their evil deed and they will out themselves eventually.

07:34 So there you have it. Dōng Chuāng Shì Fā. Season 9 is now officially off and running. Nine more beauties coming your way over the next eighteen weeks.

CHINESE SAYINGS BOOK 3
EPISODE 24

07:44 | Thanks everyone for tuning it. This is Laszlo Montgomery signing off as usual from Los Angeles in the state of confusion. Please find it in your heart to join me again next time for another exciting episode of the Chinese Sayings Podcast.

Chinese Sayings Book 3 Episode 25

R-E-S-P-E-C-T

程门立雪—Chéng Mén Lì Xuě

TRANSCRIPT

00:00 | Hey everyone, Laszlo Montgomery here with a nice new Chinese Saying for you at the podcast show that has stayed true to its name since 2016, The Chinese Sayings Podcast. And since 2023 at least, it's also available on the very same podcast RSS feed where you can find the China History Podcast.

00:21 | Today's chéngyǔ is one of those that deals with the feelings of respect a student has for their teacher and while the story isn't the same, it sort of reminded me of that scene near the end of Zhāng Yìmóu 张艺谋 1999 film, The Road Home. Wǒde Fùqīn Mǔqīn 我的父親母親. Every time I see that movie I have to keep a box of tissues close by for that tearjerker of an ending.

00:46 | So this is a much different story with a different ending, but there's some similarity in the emotional feelings of reverence some feel or have felt for teachers who meant a lot to us.

CHINESE SAYINGS BOOK 3
EPISODE 25

01:01 | Chéng Mén Lì Xuě. Let's pick it apart and see what it literally says.

01:05 | Chéng 程 has a whole bunch of meanings, but in this chengyu it's the surname of two of the characters.

01:11 | Mén 门 is a door, entrance or gate.

01:15 | Lì 立 means to stand and xuě 雪 means the snow.

01:19 | Chéng's door stand snow. On the face if it, those four characters aren't terribly helpful in revealing the meaning. So you know what that means. We'll have to tell the story behind these four syllables and then everything will be as clear as rain.

01:37 | Like more than a few past sayings featured on this podcast show, this one comes to us direct from the Book of Sòng, the Sòng Shū 宋书 that was compiled during the succeeding Yuán dynasty. And it stars the Northern Song philosopher, literary figure and upright official, Yáng Shí 杨时.

01:56 | Besides his service to the government, Yáng Shí's also remembered as a student of the renowned brothers Chéng Hào 程颢 and Chéng Yí 程颐. Together with Yóu Zuò 游酢, Lǚ Dàlín 吕大临, and Xiè Liángzuǒ 谢良佐, he was known as one of the four major disciples of the Chéngs, the Chéngmén sìdà dìzǐ 程门四大弟子.

02:18 | Chéng Hào and Chéng Yí, the Chéng Brothers, were two of the Five Founders of Neo-Confucianism in the

CHINESE SAYINGS BOOK 3
EPISODE 25

Sòng. And they are both extremely revered for their contributions to this Sòngxué 宋学 as it came to be known in Chinese, Sòng Studies. They didn't call it Neo-Confucianism. Come to think of it, they didn't even call Confucianism Confucianism.

02:42　I spoke at length about the Chéng Brothers in the History of Chinese Philosophy series, some of you may recall.

02:49　So, Yáng Shí, was this remarkable scholar and writer of prose who, like a few of the greatest scholar-literati throughout Chinese history exhibited so much talent at an early age. As he grew older, he threw himself even more whole-heartedly into the study of history and philosophy.

03:12　Then in the year 1076, at only twenty-three years of age, during the time of Song Emperor Shénzōng 神宗, he placed first in the imperial civil service examinations, earning his jìnshì 进士 degree.

03:23　This was highly unusual and quite a remarkable achievement as most aspirants to the civil bureaucracy didn't earn a jìnshì degree till well into their thirties and forties. It was by far the most difficult degree to obtain but if you passed, and especially if your score ranked near the top, you were guaranteed a nice future and a plum position in the government.

03:46　After obtaining his jìnshì degree, Yáng Shí could have had his pick of any official position. But rather than take advantage of the situation he found himself in, he turned

CHINESE SAYINGS BOOK 3
EPISODE 25

down all the offers and chose instead to stay where he was and continue to further his learning.

04:02 He travelled to Luòyáng, in Hénán Province, where the famous Neo-Confucian scholar Chéng Hào lived. Chéng Hào agreed to take on Yáng Shí as a student, and the two of them lived together as student and teacher in the greatest of harmony until 1081, when Yáng Shí took his leave of Chéng Hào to return to the south of China. As Chéng Hào watched his protégé depart, he remarked contentedly, 'Now I feel sure that my ideas will spread even to the far South!'

04:36 Four years later in 1085, Yáng Shí received word of Chéng Hào's death. This of course was devastating news and to honor his revered teacher, despite their lack of actual kinship, he set up an ancestral shrine for Chéng Hào in his own family home.

04:54 Later on when Yáng Shí was about forty years old, he decided to pursue further education and went to seek a master with an equal reputation to his former teacher. The natural choice was of course Chéng Hào's younger brother, Chéng Yí.

05:12 Brothers they were, but Chéng Hào and Chéng Yí had one profound and fundamental difference in their Confucian thought. And it revolved around their interpretation of the Confucian concept of lǐ 理 and qì 气, which can be translated as principle and vital energy, respectively.

CHINESE SAYINGS BOOK 3
EPISODE 25

Chéng Hào, he believed in the innate goodness of human nature. But younger brother Chéng Yí, he believed human nature was a dichotomy of good and evil, and he emphasized the importance of cultivating one's moral character to overcome all these innate tendencies we all come pre-loaded with that lead us towards wrongdoing.

05:55 Anyway, Yáng Shí and his traveling companion who also sought out Chéng Yì as his teacher, made that long journey north to Hénán province to that most ancient and consequential city of Luòyáng. And in the dead of winter, with a heavy snow falling, they finally made it Chéng Yí's front gate. Just as they were about to announce themselves, they quickly learned that Chéng Yí right at that time, happened to be taking an afternoon siesta. Not wanting to disturb the master's rest, Yáng Shí and his friend stood as still as statues outside his door, where the snow was continuing to fall thick and fast. And there they waited patiently.

06:41 By the time Chéng Yí awoke, a foot of snow had gathered, and when he opened his door and saw these two would-be students standing quietly outside, covered head-to-toe in snow, he quickly invited them in and welcomed them.

06:55 And this story from the Book of Sòng is often trotted out whenever one wants to point to someone's dedication to scholarship and for the respect a student has for their master or teacher.

07:09 The essence of that respect is manifested in this four character saying Chéng Mén Lì Xuě. Standing in the snow outside Master Chéng's door. This is a chengyu that describes someone extremely dedicated to the pursuit of scholarship and who is extremely respectful and reverential of their teachers.

07:30　Just like that ending in the Zhāng Yìmóu film. The son thought, who would honor his mother's demand that his father, a school teacher for his whole life, who taught in a small village in rural Shǎnxī 陕西, receive a traditional burial. The son didn't think anyone would bother to show up to help carry his father's coffin all the way home from the city where he had died, back to his village. But in the end, hundreds of his former students, upon hearing the news of their teacher's passing, came from all over the country to show their respect for their teacher. In a way, you can say they all came to Chéngmén Lìxuě.

08:09　Chéng Mén Lì Xuě. The great scholar literatus Yáng Shí, rather than disturb the rest of this revered and celebrated Neo-Confucian philosopher teacher Chéng Yí, elected to stand before his door in the cold, covered in snow until his teacher awoke from his afternoon rest.

08:31　Some of us might not have much use for this chéngyǔ. But for those who are perhaps in academia or who went through school and remember some of the people who educated them, we can recall this story of Yáng Shí and how he Chéng Mén Lì Xuě rather than disturb his teacher's afternoon slumber.

CHINESE SAYINGS BOOK 3
EPISODE 25

08:50 So, Chéng Mén Lì Xuě. Remember that one when you need a phrase to describe the reverence and respect either yourself or someone else exhibits for a teacher. I've had a few myself whose doors I'd gladly stand before in the falling snow, rather than disturb or inconvenience them.

09:09 And that's going to be it my fine friends. This is Laszlo Montgomery signing off from Los Angeles, California. Do think about coming back again next time for another exciting episode of the Chinese Sayings Podcast.

**Chinese Sayings Book 3
Episode 26**

HAD ENOUGH YET?

七擒孟获—Qī Qín Mèng Huò

TRANSCRIPT

00:00	Greetings everyone, all over the world, Laszlo Montgomery here again with another Chinese Sayings Podcast.
00:08	Today we're featuring one of the many stories that are part of the legends and lore contained in Chinese history. Qī Qín Mèng Huò. This is the story of the 3rd century AD Southern Mán 南蛮 leader Mèng Huò 孟获 and all his many run-ins with the Chinese history Hall of Famer from the Shǔ Kingdom 蜀国, Zhūgě Liàng 诸葛亮.
00:32	The tale of Qī Qín Mèng Huò 七擒孟获 comes to us from the Romance of the Three Kingdoms, Luó Guànzhōng's 罗贯中 14th century novel of those events leading up to and during the Three Kingdoms era from 220-280.
00:46	Let's break the chéngyǔ down into its constituent parts.
00:49	Qī Qín Mèng Huò.

195

 CHINESE SAYINGS BOOK 3
EPISODE 26

00:52 | Qī 七 is the number seven.

00:55 | Qín 擒 means to capture.

00:59 | And as I just said, Mèng Huò 孟获 was a tribal leader of a non-Hàn Chinese indigenous people from the Yangzi River Valleys.

01:05 | There's some scholarly speculation that these Nán Mán 南蛮, Southern Mán people are the forebears of today's Yí People 彝族, but can't yet say for sure. Because of their geographical proximity, the Southern Mán were a constant irritant to the Kingdom of Chǔ 楚国 during the Warring States Period.

01:25 | So Qī Qín Mèng Huò, Seven capture Mèng Huò. Everyone who knows the story, knows what this means. But being for the benefit of Mr. Kite, here's the tale of Mèng Huò in the mid 3rd Century.

01:41 | This is one of those things that probably never happened. Whether Mèng Huò was actually captured and released seven times is heavily doubted by historians, but the dramatization of Mèng Huò's eventual surrender to Zhūgě Liàng has nevertheless become an oft-told story from those times.

02:01 | It all started when the Shǔ king Liu Bèi 刘备 died in 223. Cáo Pī 曹丕, son of Cáo Cāo 曹操, and the ruler of the Wèi kingdom 魏国 had cut a deal with these Southern Mán and together with other tribes in the southwest of China and his own Wèi army, he kept the pressure up on

CHINESE SAYINGS BOOK 3
EPISODE 26

Zhūgě Liàng and the Shǔ Kingdom.

02:24 Mèng Huò, as I said, was a leader of the Southern Mán tribes who bordered Shǔ. These barbarian tribes, as they were referred to in the official histories, took this opportunity of Liú Bèi's passing to rebel against Shǔ control. Zhūgě Liàng therefore had to lead forces to subdue them.

02:44 The first time Zhūgě Liàng captured Mèng Huò in battle, he had used a ruse of having two of his generals pretend to be defeated in battle. The aim was to lure Mèng Huò's forces into chasing after them, straight into a narrow valley where they were then caught in a pincer formation and surrounded on all sides by Zhūgě Liàng's forces. Mèng Huò was captured alive by Shǔ soldiers. However, when he was brought before Zhūgě Liàng, this defiant leader was spitting nickels and said, "You didn't catch me fair and square — you lured me into a trap. Do you think for even one second that I will meekly surrender to you?"

03:27 Zhūgě Liàng laughed and allowed Mèng Huò to go without even a warning or any further thought.

03:33 After Mèng Huò 'escaped', air quotes around that word escape, he rallied the remnants of his troops and charged Zhūgě Liàng's camp again. He was again captured alive and brought before Zhūgě Liàng. This time, he yelled, "If you're a real man, let me go back and gather a real army, and then meet me in battle and see if you can defeat me."

03:57   Zhūgě Liàng again laughed, and smiled, "Yeah right," and he let Mèng Huò go for a second time.

04:04   For his third attempt, Mèng Huò tried to use cunning against Zhūgě Liàng. He had his younger brother pretend to surrender to Zhūgě Liàng and bring him rich gifts, with secret orders to assassinate Zhūgě Liàng. But Zhūgě Liàng didn't trust this sudden envoy surrendering so easily and bearing gifts. He had all their wine secretly laced with sleeping medicine. Then, when Mèng Huò and a force of thirty thousand Southern Mán fighters barged into the Shǔ camp, expecting to find the camp in turmoil, Zhūgě Liàng dead, and the preemptive barbarian forces already engaged in battle, they instead found their allies all fast asleep and the Shǔ forces ready to capture them.

04:52   Thus Mèng Huò was captured a third time, but he still railed against Zhūgě Liàng, saying that his plan had only failed because his younger brother had too much fondness for drink. So Zhūgě Liàng let him go a third time.

05:08   Mèng Huò left and rallied some allies among other indigenous tribes. They decided to attack the Shǔ camp with a force ten-thousand strong, all decked out in barbarian fashion with war paint and loose hair. Mèng Huò himself donned rhinoceros-skin armor and rode on a red bull.

05:29   Although the Shǔ forces were initially terrified at this frightful onslaught, Zhūgě Liàng knew that the Shǔ

CHINESE SAYINGS BOOK 3
EPISODE 26

defenses were enough to withstand the initial assault, so he ordered his forces to hide behind their camp barriers and not to engage until Mèng Huò's company had worn themselves out.

05:49 They did this and won a decisive battle. Mèng Huò himself managed to escape and collect himself, when he suddenly saw Zhūgě Liàng's chariot approaching. In a fit of rage, he charged at Zhūgě Liàng, trying to take him prisoner. But in his rage he failed to see a ditch between them, which he tripped and fell into. Thus he was captured for the fourth time. He shook his angry fist at the ditch that had tripped him, and Zhūgě Liàng released him for a fourth time.

06:16 Mèng Huò then tried to seek aid from a nearby barbarian warlord who had once risen in rebellion. But the warlord had been defeated in battle by Zhūgě Liàng before. He was extremely grateful to Zhūgě Liàng for not killing his entire clan as he had a right to do. So, to show his sincerity, he caught Mèng Huò himself and had him brought to Zhūgě Liàng. Of course, Mèng Huò did not consider this fair play and was released a fifth time.

06:44 This time, Mèng Huò sought as an ally a nearby chief of one of the many tribes in the area who was known to wield snake-charming magic. In a mark of growing desperation, he even sent his wife out into battle against Zhūgě Liàng, and she was surprisingly effective, wielding throwing knives and capturing two Shǔ generals.

07:07 But Zhūgě Liàng had preempted the snake attack and

was able to fend off the snakes with fire, eventually winning the battle. However, he did not capture Mèng Huò in battle. Mèng Huò, thinking to strike by subterfuge again, secretly armed his forces with concealed weapons and entered the Shǔ camp, pretending to surrender.

07:30 But Zhūgě Liàng of course did not trust this surrender and had Mèng Huò's company stopped and searched before they could venture far enough into the Shǔ camp to do any damage. Mèng Huò said, "You have captured me again, but only on the seventh time will I consider myself truly defeated." So, without even being granted an audience with Zhūgě Liàng, he was let go a sixth time.

07:56 Mèng Huò decided to lead one final assault against the Shǔ forces with another barbarian ally. Predictably he was again defeated and captured. But this time, true to his word, Mèng Huò acknowledged that he had been bested. After being captured a seventh time, Mèng Huò never dared to rise against the Shǔ again, and in fact was instrumental in convincing many other tribes of the region to surrender to the Shǔ, thus solidifying their control over their borders.

08:30 Qī Qín Mèng Huò, seven times capturing Mèng Huò. This Chinese Saying is used to describe a strategic retreat when victory seems certain. When you Qī Qín Mèng Huò you are letting the enemy off with almost exaggerated easiness in order to win their heartfelt surrender.

08:51 In the last century, this chengyu was written into Hán Sùyīn's 韩素音 autobiography, "My House Has Two

CHINESE SAYINGS BOOK 3
EPISODE 26

Doors" that came out in 1980. She showcased this chengyu to describe the Chinese retreat in the 1962 Sino-Indian War. She wrote,

09:10 'In November, twenty-five days after the beginning of the Chinese military reprisal, the Chinese government announced a total and unilateral military withdrawal to ten kilometers behind the McMahon Line. They stated that all weapons and ammunition captured, and all prisoners, would be returned without any compensation demanded; gave the lists of the prisoners captured—who had been treated, mainly for frostbite but also for wounds, in Chinese hospitals—and then sat down, waiting for Nehru to come to the negotiating table.'

09:45 'Many people in the world were puzzled; not least the newsmen and the agencies. How to explain what China had done? It did not fit into any known, recognized Western pattern of diplomacy. I think they began to realize that there was a Chinese way of doing things, of thinking, of acting, which need not refer to what they were told in the newspapers, and that the fascination of China resided precisely in this different way of handling situations, people, facts.

10:15 'This was, as Chou Enlai would say, a repetition of the episode "Seven Times Capture and Release Mèng Huò." None of this was reported in the Western press. But all the Chinese, whether in China, in Taiwan or in South East Asia, duly used the phrase Qī Qín Mèng Huò, and overseas Chinese of all political blends would say to each other, "Ah yes, seven times catch Mèng Huò".

CHINESE SAYINGS BOOK 3
EPISODE 26

10:46 | To let someone off easy, whether in battle or just metaphorically speaking, is to Qī Qín Mèng Huò. Anyone with knowledge of this story from the Romance of the Three Kingdoms will know what you're talking about. Seven times Mèng Huò was bested by the clever and wise Zhūgě Liàng. Seven times Mèng Huò was let off easy before he finally threw in the towel.

11:10 | Qī Qín Mèng Huò, everyone.

11:12 | Okay, that's it until next time. More good chengyu's coming, I assure you, from this long running educational program, suitable for families, as well. This is Laszlo Montgomery signing off from Los Angeles, California. Please consider coming back next time for another exciting episode of the Chinese Sayings Podcast.

Chinese Sayings Book 3
Episode 27

THE FIRST CUT IS THE DEEPEST

剪不断, 理还乱—Jiǎn Bù Duàn, Lǐ Hái Luàn

TRANSCRIPT

00:00	Hi Everyone, guess who? Yeah, me again, Laszlo Montgomery, here for you with another pretty halfway decent chengyu.
00:09	Today we're going to look at Jiǎn bù duàn, Lǐ hái luàn 剪不断 理还乱. Six characters, two more than usual but look at it this way, you're getting 50% more syllables for the price of four.
00:22	Jiǎn bù duàn, Lǐ hái luàn Let's do the usual.
00:26	Jiǎn 剪 is a scissors or as a verb it means to cut.
00:30	Bù 不 means no and duàn 断 means to cut off or break off.
00:36	Lǐ 理 among its myriad of definitions means to straighten a matter out.
00:41	Hái 还 means still or yet and luàn 乱 means chaos or a mess.

CHINESE SAYINGS BOOK 3
EPISODE 27

00:44 Cut not cut off straighten up still a mess. I guess if you're a fluent Chinese speaker you'd be able to figure this out. But this chengyu Jiǎn bù duàn, Lǐ hái luàn has a story attached to it that offers us all a nice little history lesson.

01:05 Starring in this chengyu is Lǐ Yù 李煜. Not someone who comes to mind instantly. He lived from 937 to 978. The Tang Dynasty ended in 907. So Lǐ Yù lived during the historical period that is sandwiched in between the Táng and the Sòng Dynasty. This is the Five Dynasties Ten Kingdoms Period that lasted 902-979.

01:32 Before I get to the chengyu, let me first dish on Lǐ Yù and why he was one of the more memorable characters from this chaotic time in Chinese history when the country was all divided.

01:45 And as The Romance of the Three Kingdoms foretold at the very beginning: 'The nation, long divided, must unite; and long united, must divide'. Although this famous opening line sentence refers to the chaos China suffered after the collapse of the Han dynasty in the 200s AD, it could just as well have applied seven centuries later to the Five Dynasties and Ten Kingdoms era.

02:10 The Five Dynasties and Ten Kingdoms are so named because of the succession of small nation-states that proliferated across the former imperial territories of the Tang, none of them lasting for more than a human lifespan. Many of these kingdoms named themselves after former imperial dynasties. Thus you had the Later Zhou, Southern Tang, Later Tang, etc., all desperate to

CHINESE SAYINGS BOOK 3
EPISODE 27

gain even a modicum of legitimacy by taking the name of a former central power.

02:41   The Five Dynasties and Ten Kingdoms era started coming to a close in 960 A.D., when the Song Dynasty founder, Zhào Kuāngyìn founded the Song Dynasty. After he seized the throne of one of the ten kingdoms, he began a sixteen-year campaign of reuniting all the breakaway states under a single imperial banner. This long and violent military undertaking would only conclude three years after Zhào Kuāngyìn passed in 976 A.D. We remember him as Sòng Tàizǔ.

03:17   Finally, in 979 A.D., the period of division was over. China was once again united under the Song, which would reign for the next three hundred years until the Mongols blew into town with all their shock and awe tactics.

03:33   So, Lǐ Yù, he was born into the royal family of the Southern Táng kingdom, which lasted from 937-976 A.D. As far as the Five Dynasties and Ten Kingdoms period went, the Southern Tang was a relatively stable and prosperous state. As its name suggests, it was one of the southern kingdoms further away from the chaos in the Central Plains regions. Its capital was in today's Nanjing. Since their kingdom was not a military hotspot, the Southern Tang nobility regularly hosted banquets, parties, and allotted ample time to the pursuit of the arts. The Southern Tang produced some of the most accomplished painters of ancient China, and copies of their paintings still survive today.

CHINESE SAYINGS BOOK 3
EPISODE 27

04:25 | And it was from this genteel, epicurean milieu that we get Lǐ Yù. Lǐ Yù was the sixth son of the king of Southern Tang, and, like many younger princes in Chinese history, he never gave ascending to the throne a second thought. Partly out of genuine interest, partly to show that he was no threat to his more ambitious older brothers, Lǐ Yù devoted his time to writing poetry. He became well-versed in the most popular poetic form of the time, the cí 词 or lyric poetry form — where a poet writes a set of lyrics to an already extant tune for a courtesan to sing at a banquet.

05:05 | Lǐ Yù was a poet, not a politician. He had a reputation for being weak, air-headed, and too gentle to rule. He lacked all the necessary qualities required of a leader. So, when a series of accidents and early deaths dispatched everyone in the line of succession, Lǐ Yù ended up being king.

05:25 | The Southern Tang had already lost a series of battles with neighboring kingdoms, and by the time Lǐ Yù ascended the throne in 961 A.D., it was very much a weakened vassal state, no longer a kingdom in its own right. But, as one of those less-threatening Southern kingdoms, it was allowed to exist until quite late in the Song dynasty's campaign of unification, 976 A.D., to be exact.

05:52 | And when this final blow came, one of the conditions of surrender that the Song imposed upon the Southern Tang was that its king, Lǐ Yù, be taken to the Song capital of Kaifeng in the north, and be placed under house

CHINESE SAYINGS BOOK 3
EPISODE 27

arrest. So Lǐ Yù, was condemned to live out the short remainder of his life far away from his homeland and his people. In China today, Lǐ Yù is remembered as a very mediocre ruler but a very great poet. Some have even suggested his was the greatest artistic talent of all the Chinese rulers, including even Huīzōng and Qiánlóng.

06:32 The pathos of his life story, his unwillingness to take the throne, his eventual death in exile in the Song capital, contributes not insignificantly to Lǐ Yù's reputation. One of the most hotly debated topics surrounding him is which of his poems were written before his defeat and exile, and which were written after. Since many of Lǐ Yù's poems cannot be conclusively dated, scholars are still debating whether each had been written post-exile or before.

07:04 This particular poem that is the source of this chengyu is one of the undated ones which means that, purely from historical evidence, we can't conclusively say if Lǐ Yù wrote it before or after he was placed under house arrest in Kaifeng. You'll have to judge for yourself. It's titled Xiāng Jiàn Huān 相见欢: 'The Happiness of Meeting' quite an optimistic title for such a poem containing such a desolate tone.

07:30 These Cí or 'lyric' poems weren't given titles of their own. They were just named for whatever the tune was that the poem was set to. Did Lǐ Yù intentionally choose the tune 'The Happiness of Meeting' for the tragic irony of the mismatch between poem and title? Or did he simply think these lyrics happened to sound best to that tune?

CHINESE SAYINGS BOOK 3
EPISODE 27

07:52 Whatever the context, Lǐ Yù has provided one of the most famous lines in Chinese literature, very quotable whenever you want to describe any painful emotion, but particularly the grief and pain of parting from a loved one.

08:08 This might be akin to the immortal line from act two scene two of the Shakespeare play Romeo and Juliet, when she bid Romeo farewell, "Parting is such sweet sorrow." I guess you can say Jiǎn bù duàn, Lǐ hái luàn is a Chinese version of that oft used verse from Shakespeare.

08:29 Let me read the poem and follow it up with a Stephen Owen translation from the Anthology of Chinese Literature.

08:36
Wú yán dú shàng xī lóu, Yuè rú gōu,
无言独上西楼，月如钩，
Jìmò wútóng shēnyuàn suǒ qīngqiū.
寂寞梧桐深院锁清秋。
Jiǎn bùduàn, lǐ hái luàn,
剪不断，理还乱，
shì líchóu, bié shì yībān zīwèi zài xīntóu.
是离愁，别是一般滋味在心头。

08:56
Without a word I climbed the western tower —
The moon was like a hook.
The silent yard stretched deep
Through chestnut trees, enclosing autumn,
cool and clear.
You can cut it, but never cut it through, get it set,
then it's a mess again —

CHINESE SAYINGS BOOK 3
EPISODE 27

That's the sadness of being apart.
It has a flavor all its own.

09:22   Jiǎn bùduàn, lǐ hái luàn, You can cut it, but never cut it through, get it set, then it's a mess again. A six-character Chinese saying to describe the sorrow of parting. And the key to understanding the meaning behind this chengyu is the poem by Lǐ Yù of the Southern Tang.

09:41   Jiǎn bùduàn, lǐ hái luàn everybody.

09:45   That's it. This is Laszlo Montgomery signing off from Los Angeles, California, inviting you to join me next time for another exciting episode of the Chinese Sayings Podcast.

Chinese Sayings Book 3
Episode 28

YOU CAN GET IT IF YOU REALLY WANT (BUT YOU MUST TRY)

磨杵成针—Mó Chǔ Chéng Zhēn

TRANSCRIPT

00:00	Greetings one and all, Laszlo Montgomery here. If you're just sitting down to a nice cup of tea or some other beverage, I suggest put it in a to-go cup because this one won't take long.
00:12	Today's Chinese Saying is a real good one. A great little story and still relevant in our trying times. Mó Chǔ Chéng Zhēn 磨杵成针. This one I can almost offer you a money-back guarantee that when I break these four characters down, you'll already be able to figure out what this one means.
00:30	Mó Chǔ Chéng Zhēn.
00:33	Mó 磨 means to rub, grind, wear down, or polish.
00:37	A Chǔ 杵 is a pestle, like in a mortar and pestle. It's also a metal bar or a wooden club used to beat clothes during washing.

CHINESE SAYINGS BOOK 3
EPISODE 28

00:48 | Chéng 成 means to accomplish or succeed or in this case to become.

00:53 | And the fourth character zhēn 针 is a needle.

00:57 | Grind metal bar become needle. You can already get the main idea but without knowing the gùshi 故事 or story, you can't quite fully appreciate it.

01:08 | The chūchù 出处 or source of this chengyu is a book from the late Southern Sòng called Fāng Yú Shèng Lǎn 方舆胜览, The Splendors of the Land. This came out in 1239 during the long reign of the ho-hum Emperor Lǐzōng 宋理宗. He was on duty when the Mongols ran roughshod over the Jürchens in 1234. So we all know what followed a few decades later. But this Emperor Lǐzōng, he didn't do much to address his Mongol issue and thanks to that, the Southern Song went down in flames fifteen years after the end of his reign.

01:45 | So during this frightful time, there lived a noted Confucian scholar and official of the Southern Song named Zhù Mù 祝穆. And he wrote this seventy volume work that focused on the geography and customs in the counties that were part of Lín'ān Prefecture 临安'府. And Lín'ān of course was the capital of the Song and in its day, 12th-13th century, I've seen this in more than a few places, it had the highest population and ranked among the largest cities in the world. This is in the vicinity of present day Hangzhou in fabulous Zhèjiāng province.

CHINESE SAYINGS BOOK 3
EPISODE 28

02:23   And contained in this work, The Splendors of the Land, is this story from which we get this very useful chengyu, Mó Chǔ Chéng Zhēn. It comes from a chapter on the city of Méizhōu 眉州, in today's Sichuan Province, just south of the provincial capital of Chengdu. Today it's called Méishān 眉山. The histories mention that the great poet Lǐ Bái 李白 spent many years there as a child, attending school.

02:54   And Lǐ Bái, who lived 701-762, along with the poet Dù Fǔ 杜甫, are considered China's two most celebrated and renowned poets. Lǐ Bái was known as the Shīxiān 诗仙 or Poet Immortal and Dù Fǔ, the Shīshèng 诗圣, or Poet Sage.

03:12   Lǐ Bái was an avid Taoist and a lover of wine, and both influences can be seen in much of his poetry. According to legend, and as written in Zhù Mù's book, Lǐ Bái, in his childhood, was sent to school near Elephant Ear Mountain in Méizhōu, again today's Méishān. As a young'n, Lǐ Bái was an exceptionally clever child and it took him only two or three repetitions to memorize information which it took others ten repetitions to learn.

03:43   Like many fast learners and geniuses who came before and after Lǐ Bái, the teaching pace was way too slow for him and he grew lazy and restless. He would often play hooky from school and go exploring around Elephant Ear Mountain.

03:59   Tradition has it that one day, as Lǐ Bái was playing by a creek in the mountain, he came across an old white-

CHINESE SAYINGS BOOK 3
EPISODE 28

haired pópo 婆婆 filing this rather large iron rod as big as her arm against a slab of river rock. Lǐ Bái stared incredulously at the old woman as she ground that thick iron rod back and forth against the rough stone, wearing it down no doubt, but not visibly. It all seemed so pointless.

04:30 So young Lǐ Bái watched her for a while and eventually his curiosity got the best of him and Lǐ Bái asked the old pópo, "Why are you filing down that iron rod? What use could it possibly be?" She replied, "I am filing it down to make an embroidery needle." Lǐ Bái said, "But, at the rate you're going, that will take forever!"

04:51 The old woman thereupon replied to Lǐ Bái with these immortal lines that have been repeated millions of times throughout the centuries following the Song Dynasty, Zhǐyào gōngfū shēn, tiěchǔ Mó chéngzhēn 只要功夫深，铁杵磨成针 "If you work hard enough, you can grind an iron bar into a needle. With enough time and work, it will be done in the end."

05:16 Lǐ Bái let that sink in and continued to watch with respect and admiration at the lǎo pópo's single-minded determination to make an embroidery needle out of that thick iron rod. This inspired young Lǐ Bái profoundly. From that day on, he applied himself and worked hard at school, no longer using his innate cleverness as an excuse to skip class and not pay attention. He devoted himself to learning and in nurturing his creative abilities. It was due to his hard work and perseverance that he was eventually able to become one of the greatest poets of China.

CHINESE SAYINGS BOOK 3
EPISODE 28

05:58 | As for the old woman, her surname was Wǔ (武), and in honour of her memory and her great service to the poet Lǐ Bái, there is a rock at the spot at where tradition says she met him. It's called named Wǔ Shì Yán 武氏岩 or Madame Wǔ's Rock.

06:15 | Mó chǔ chéng zhēn, to file an iron rod into a needle. With enough perseverance, even the most impossible task can be accomplished. If you put your mind to any task that lies ahead, and you give it your all, you too can grind an iron bar down to a needle.

06:35 | We were all taught that Rome wasn't built in a day and that practice makes perfect and slow and steady wins the race. It was hammered into some of us that little strokes fell great oaks. Inch by inch, anything's a cinch. And that if at first you don't succeed, try, try, try again. You get the main idea.

06:56 | Let's all learn a lesson from the old woman in Méizhōu who Móchǔ 磨杵, who filed that iron bar in order to chéngzhēn 成针, turn it into a needle. Móchǔ chéngzhēn.

07:09 | See, I told you this one would be short. And until the next time, my good-looking listeners, this is Laszlo Montgomery signing off once again from the capital of the Southland, Los Angeles, California. Please consider coming back next time for another exciting episode of the Chinese Sayings Podcast.

Chinese Sayings Book 3 Episode 29

FINISHED BEHIND THE LAST PLACE GUY

名落孙山—Míng Luò Sūn Shān

TRANSCRIPT

00:00 | Greetings everyone, all over this warming world, Laszlo Montgomery here with the season 9 closer. Hard to believe we've already reached the end. These twenty weeks sure flew by. I'd like to thank every one of you for listening and for your support.

00:17 | We're going to end things on an amusing note. Today's offering is a funny little story that comes to us from the Song Dynasty. The source of the chéngyǔ is a little-known work by the literary figure Fàn Gōngchēng 范公偁 called the Guòtínglù 过庭录.

00:33 | But before we get into all that, let's break down the four characters for today's featured Chinese Saying, Míng Luò Sūn Shān 名落孙山.

00:41 | A míng 名 is a name. What is your míng, what is your name.

00:46 | And luò 落 has a whole bunch of meanings but in this

	case it means to lower or fall behind or below.
00:52	And Sūn Shān 孙山? Well, he's the main character from this story.
00:56	Míng Luò Sūn Shān. Name fall behind Sūn Shān. Who knows what that means. Could be anything. So let's hear the gùshi 故事 or story behind the saying which will clearly reveal the meaning behind these seemingly four unrelated characters. Míng Luò Sūn Shān.
01:15	So, sometime in the mid to late 11th Century there lived this happy-go-lucky young man named Sūn Shān. He was sort of the jokester in his village in the Jiāngnán 江南 region and some of the older folks used to call him a Huájī Cáizǐ 滑稽才子. Huájī 滑稽 was similar to Xiàngsheng 相声 cross-talk that was popular in the north. Huájī was more of a Shanghai-Hangzhou-Suzhou kind of thing.
01:42	He aspired to rise above his station in life and had studied for the imperial civil service exams. And when the time came to head to the capital to sit for the exams, his father and everyone saw him off and wished him well. Accompanying Sūn Shān was another lad from his village who was tagging along to also sit for the exam. Off they went to the capital to go regurgitate all they had memorized through relentless study of the classics.
02:14	After the exam was all finished the two aspiring scholar officials went to the announcement board where all the test results were posted. Sūn Shān started at the top of

CHINESE SAYINGS BOOK 3
EPISODE 29

	the list and worked his way down until finally, he saw his name listed dead last on the roster of passing grades.
02:34	Well, even though he finished last, at least he made the list and breathed a sigh of relief. However the fellow villager who came with him was sorely disappointed to see that he didn't even make the list. He failed in the exam and didn't get a passing grade. This meant he either had to take the exam again or resign himself to an ordinary life, either working on the family farm or some other humdrum career.
03:01	Sūn Shān took off back to the village by himself and when he approached the gate, his father eagerly awaited him and welcomed him home. And then he asked his son the big question. Well, did he pass or not.
03:15	And Sūn Shān replied that he passed but had finished in last place. His father shrugged but nonetheless felt a sense of relief that his son had been a lucky man who made the grade.
03:28	Then the other young man's father came forward and also eagerly and hopefully asked Sūn Shān, "And what about my son? How did he do?"
03:36	And here is where the chengyu appears. When Sūn Shān gave this father the news, not wanting to cause any loss of face to the man, he replied that, well, he himself had finished in last place and as for the son, Míng Luò Sūn Shān.

219

CHINESE SAYINGS BOOK 3
EPISODE 29

03:54 | Before all the assembled villagers anxious to see if any of their own had met with success, Sūn Shān, to preserve the face of the father and put the disappointing news inside a less unpleasant wrapper, allowed the father to know, by his response, his son had failed.

04:12 | But rather than coming out straightaway and say his son failed, by uttering the words Míng Luò Sūn Shān, the results were clear. Sun Shan finished last and the other young man's name was below Sūn Shān's. In other words, not on the list. By framing the response like he did, he let the father down a little more gently than simply announcing his son's scholastic failure.

04:39 | So this chengyu, Míng Luò Sūn Shān, can be taken down off the shelf to mean someone failed in their goal. If your child didn't pass the Gāokǎo college entrance exam, there's no need to rub it in and say he, she, or they failed. It's enough to just say Míng Luò Sūn Shān. For a scholarship award, a promotion, or any kind of competition. If it didn't work out in their favor, Míng Luò Sūn Shān.

05:07 | That's a milder way of saying they were met with failure, or giving them the thumbs down sign. Just say those four syllables, Míng Luò Sūn Shān, and the meaning is clear. No one needs to bow their head in shame.

05:21 | Okay, that's gonna be it I'm afraid. Time flies when you're having fun. We now bring down the curtain on Season 9. As usual I'm gonna take a little time off to chill, and you can be sure I'll be back in a reasonable amount

CHINESE SAYINGS BOOK 3
EPISODE 29

of time with ten more episodes for you.

05:39 That's it all, you beautiful and intelligent CSP listeners. Thanks so much for your listenership all season long. Thanks to all of you who subscribed to my Patreon, CHP Premium, gave me SuperThanks on my YouTube channel. My deepest thanks. Please join me again next season for more exciting episodes of the Chinese Sayings Podcast.

ABOUT THE AUTHOR

Laszlo Montgomery is the creator and presenter of the China History Podcast, and other Chinese culture related podcasts. He began his Chinese studies in 1979 at the University of Illinois, and lived in Hong Kong between 1989-1998. He has helped Chinese companies build market share in the US, and in 2010, launched The China History Podcast as a channel to allow a more mass, non-academic audience to enjoy the delights of Chinese history. Originally intended for a US audience, today more than half of the show's listeners are outside the States. Cathay Pacific Airways has carried Laszlo's content on their inflight entertainment system since 2017. Laszlo has spoken frequently at universities and high schools about his love for Chinese history and culture.

www.ingramcontent.com/pod-product-compliance
Lightning Source LLC
LaVergne TN
LVHW061046070526
838201LV00074B/5190